FUELLED

BENNY STEVENS

With thanks to our corporate Kickstarters:

Darling Downs Drilling

BBR Transport

MAX SPECIALIST LIFTING EQUIPMENT HIRE TRANSPORT

GENIE EXHAUSTS WA
Since 1981

Bakers Creek
HARVESTING

ABP Freighters

Leave It To Us Landscaping

Thank you for your generous support, which made the publishing of Fuelled possible.

To our Kickstarters:

Aaron Davies	David Sullivan
Aaron Maynard	Denise & Paul Downe
Ajay Hammer	Don Bowman
Amanda Martin	Doug Green
Andrew & Michelle Katavatis	Drew Menzies
Brad Whittaker	Edmund Forman
Brenden Reardon	Emilio Russo
Brett Baile	Erin Patrick
Brett Schy	Evelyne Scholz
Brian Dickman	Gerry Stevens
Brian Hotker	Glen Learmonth
Brian Williams	Graeme Ashley
Brock Neilson	Graham Pitts
Bronson Dunne	Ian & Sonja Board
Bruce Mott	Ian Read
Celeste Daly	Jasmine Murphy
Chloe Park	Jeff Noonan
Chris Mahony	Jennifer Lingo
Chris Pobjoy	Jessica Mullins
Chris Porter	Jodie Coates
Craig Head	John Harney
Dale Gummow	John & Josie Zahra
Darling Downs Drilling	Jon Ferguson
David & Jill Falzon	Josh Wharmby

Judy Graham
Julie Bailey
Katherine Stevens
Kerry Williams
Kris Hastie
Kyarna Harrison
Mark Kuhn
Mark Rothwell
Michael Rimming
Mick Ball
Netty Packard
Nick Panagopoulos
Paige Salmeri
Paul & Julie Nieuwhof
Peter Peirano
Peter Vanderaa
Peter Warrell
Phil Luyer
Phill Paton
Ray Le-Cocq
Robyn Butler
Ron & Patricia Hogben
Ross & Majella Zammit
S Hansen

Sam Parker
Scott Wilson
Scotty McKenzie
Shane Eriksson
Steve McGuinness
Stuart Rowland
Supercharged40
Swichon Inc
Tamara Quigg
Tara Zammit
Tauri Venesia Daly
Terry Stacy
Tony, Gillian & Chris Argentino
Toohey
Toxic Cauliflour
Traci Salmeri
Travis Blentweyne
Vince Hutcheson
Warwick Taylor
Wayne & Lisa Keys
Weston Racing
Zoe Nieuwhof

Thank you for your contributions, big and small, to make this book a reality.

Copyright © Benny Stevens, 2019

All rights reserved. No part of this book may be reproduced in any form, by any electronic or mechanical means, including information storage and retrieval systems, without permission in writing from the publisher, except by a reviewer who may quote brief passages in a review.

First Edition

Acknowledgements: Thanks to Kim Stevens, Hilary Stevens, Jodie Coates, Paul Nieuwhof, Phil Luyer, Tara Zammit and Chancey Smith for their valuable support.

Dedicated to

Kevin George Stevens
25/9/1934 - 22/1/1995

Valda Lydia Stevens
23/4/1934 - 23/10/2013

David Falzon
12/5/1954 - 10/10/2018

Brett Schy
26/1/1978 - 8/6/2019

Contents

FUEL FOR THOUGHT - I 1
ROLE MODELS 3
YOUNG BLOOD 17
GROWTH 23
ON WHEELS 29
LIFE AT HIGH SPEED 35
WARNING SIGNS 45
FREESTYLER 53
FIGHT OF MY LIFE 61
DOUBTERS AND DYSFUNCTION 71
FUEL FOR THOUGHT - II 85
MOVING ON 87
FIRST STRIKE 93
TOO MUCH FUN 103
SWISS CHEESE 113
CHOPPED 129
FUEL FOR THOUGHT - III 145
NITRO 147
MY BROTHER'S KEEPER 165
REALISING RECOVERY 177
LIVING THE DREAM 191
FINISH LINE 203
FUEL FOR THOUGHT - IV 207

Fuel for Thought - I
Prologue

I watched disaster unfold from high up. My friends looked on as the ramp disappeared beneath me and I sailed over any chance of a safe landing. The ground rushed up to meet me and I could see the exact point where I was going to hit. The jump seemed to take an age and I could almost feel the pain and hear my bones breaking before that final, inevitable impact. Breaking free of gravity's constraints for a brief moment, I was committed to both the jump and the consequences that followed.

To make a motorbike fly, the rider must accelerate to a steady speed and commit to a ramp that will give them the trajectory for their stunt. I believe my life choices are a series of stunts, each with a reward for landing safely or pain if I miss. I make my decisions in the run-up, where I must choose how high I want to fly and what chances I want to take. It's a decision that is the culmination of my experiences, my upbringing and the people who have been close to me.

I have the option to stay conservative and safe, or I can aim for a stunt that is new and exciting. I don't even have to jump at all if I want my life to be boring and predictable. The safe option will likely see me landing without incident, whereas the riskier decisions could be a more difficult landing – but if I do land well then I am a champion. It's about reward versus risk.

Gravity is the same as reality, omnipotent and inescapable. Reality always brings me down – no matter how high I soar. I can land comfortably and reap the excitement of my daring decisions, or I can come crashing down to earth. Sometimes I do everything right and then have a mechanical failure rob me of the glory – the circumstances of life are like that sometimes; the wheels just fall off. People like to say 'If you're going to be dumb, you've got to be tough'. I prefer this:

Sometimes you win, sometimes you learn.

Most people think I am positively minded, but I am the opposite. I expect the worst – I know reality is like gravity, always ready to meet me, but what am I going to do? I prepare for the worst, I deal with the worst when it arrives, and I move on to the next stunt. The worst of life doesn't stop me from pursuing the highs because the lows are there regardless. Some people choose to ignore it; I choose to acknowledge the presence of the worst and treat it with disdain.

Look the devil in the eye.

Role Models

I was three years old when I first experienced for myself the thrill of speed followed by the sobering realisation of a mistake.

Dad had a Kawasaki KLF300 four-wheeler he rode around the nursery – a workhorse, not a toy – but when I watched this magical machine drive I could only see fun. Each day Dad parked the quad at the back of Nanna's house, where he stopped for morning tea, and I watched closely to see how he brought the mechanical beast to life; I only had to wait for my window of opportunity. When child and quad were left alone for a brief moment, I climbed on to the seat and followed the routine I had watched my father perform: push the button, twist the handle and pull the gear lever up. My head snapped back as the quad took off, accelerating along the driveway towards rows of neatly organised plants. Dad heard the crack of the throttle and sprinted out of the house, but I was already out of reach. "Stop, Benny! Stop!" Dad yelled.

Why would I stop? I was having way too much fun and the quad didn't scare me, I found it exhilarating. I looked back at Dad and laughed in excitement as dirt crunched underneath the tyres and the air rushed past me. I turned around to face the front of the quad again, but only just in time to see the fence I was about to smash through. The short ride didn't teach me that quads and bikes were dangerous, only that they were a means to the inducement of adrenaline.

My grandfather Kevin Stevens was born on a kitchen table at the back of a fish and chips shop in 1934, half Macedonian but raised in Perth. Grandad and Nanna Valda had their first son, my father Gary, in 1960 and his brother Kim followed in 1962.

Grandad loved plants the way I love motorbikes; they were his overwhelming passion in life. He started his first nursery in South Perth with a simple shadehouse, before moving further away from the city to Bentley, where he built a glasshouse on a larger scale. He wanted to expand his business further and so he bought land in Canning Vale in 1970. That area is now booming with light industrial and residential estates, but at the time Canning Vale was the perfect place for a nursery, with cheap land close to Perth's centre. Each year Grandad bought more land to grow the nursery and the business was christened as Canning Plant Farm. His passion proved good for business and the nursery developed a reputation for quality. It was never the biggest nursery in Australia, not even close, but it was known for growing high-quality stock.

Grandad specialised in indoor plants, he loved growing those, but there were all kinds of conifers and shrubs he added to his repertoire. He was the first grower to bring poinsettias to Australia and he sold out of the bright red plants each year. Grandad also had a passion for breeding Murray Grey cows, and he even won a Grand Champion award for one of his heifers.

Dad married my mother Gerry in 1984 and I was born on December 26, 1986, the first of three kids. My sister Jodi and brother Luke followed. For us, the nursery was home, work and play all rolled into one. Some of my earliest memories

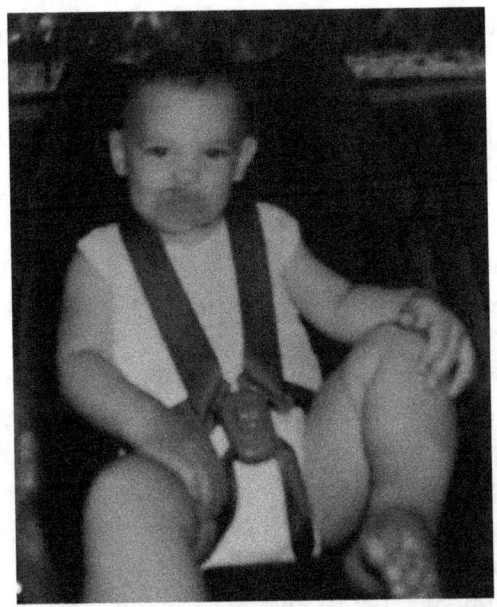

A good looking young rooster, even back then.

were of riding around the nursery on the quads, stopping in for visits at my grandparents' house. It was a great way to grow up and the men and women who worked at the nursery were like family to me. My childhood felt a little restricted socially because the nursery was not near other housing, and it was too far to ride my bicycle to see friends. But I didn't notice this isolation much at the time, because I had everything I wanted.

I was difficult to manage as a child; I was adventurous and a real smart-ass. The nursery offered a young and curious mind many types of trouble to get into and I went on many adventures, exploring the reaches of the nursery and beyond. I was all about pushing boundaries and when I was a young boy my boundaries were mostly found on foot.

One of my escapades as a four-year-old took me out of the

nursery and into the Fraser Garden Centre further down the road, where I had a good old time for the day. When my absence was noticed, the whole nursery came to a halt to look for me. The big water tanks and dam were searched, and the family were petrified they were going to find me drowned. My Uncle Kim dived for 15 minutes in the pitch black of a water tank to look for me in case I had decided on a swim. I had actually found a tractor, where I was playing in the seat until the owners of the Fraser Garden Centre discovered me. I remember feeling excited at seeing a group of quads coming from our nursery, riding over piles of soil to find me, because I thought they were coming to play too. Then I found out I was in trouble.

Dad put me on the back of his quad and took me home. He made me stand watch while he picked a branch from a silver birch tree and gave me a hiding from hell. In the relief of finding me alive he wanted to give me a painful lesson, and Mum got in lots of trouble too for not noticing I was gone. I was just an adventurous kid. Unfortunately, Dad would fly off the handle with severe punishments that often crossed the line of what was reasonable.

I was heavily influenced by the family I grew up with around the nursery. Most people only have one or two strong role models in their lives, but I had five or six and I took personality traits from each of them. The environment was work hard, play harder, and it's a wonder we all survived. All of the Stevens men, and many of our close family and friends, were shit stirrers and my earliest memories involve their behaviour around the nursery. The crazy and wild nature of my family life played a definitive role in shaping my personality today.

Grandad started the tradition of pranks. He would drape the chain of a gate over an electric fence to give a zap to anyone who tried to open it, and he convinced people to relieve themselves on the same electric fence. He hid rubber snakes and spiders in the nursery's soil bins to scare the ladies who potted his plants, and he would slam his shovel down on the concrete to make his workers jump. Grandad was the original prankster and the apples didn't fall far from the tree.

Grandad was an honest and kind man, but also tough. One night, he was eating dinner with a buyer from the nursery and was joined by Uncle Kim. Kim kept pinching Nanna Val's homemade chips from Grandad's plate. "If you do that again, I will stab you," Grandad said.

"You're too slow," Kim mocked. He went for another chip and Grandad put a fork right through his son's arm, sending Kim to hospital.

Thankfully Nanna Val was always there to be a softer influence. She was one of the kindest people I knew and if ever I had a problem she would take me in with open arms. She helped me a lot when I was growing up and taught me some very good lessons. If ever there was problem with Dad, I knew I could go to her and she would be there for me.

Nanna Val might even be where the family's revhead genes come from. There was a railway line that crossed a road near the nursery, creating a raised hump that Nanna used as a jump. Us kids would be piled inside her AMG Mercedes and she would accelerate to 140kph or more and hit the jump; I used to love it! We called her Leadfoot Nanna.

Dad had a different personality to Grandad and Nanna Val. He loved being the centre of attention and it was difficult for anyone to tell him what to do. He was proud and had trouble asking for help, tending to get caught up on small issues and holding grudges when he didn't get his own way. But like Grandad, he enjoyed shit stirring people relentlessly.

I vividly remember Dad walking into the shed at the nursery and lighting up a roman candle firework, shooting at all the workers. Everybody ducked for cover as balls of fire ricocheted through the shed. One of the nursery's longest employees, Trev, loved egging Dad on and offered to stand as a target for a roman candle firing squad, putting on overalls and plastic safety glasses and then letting the family line him up to take shots. I don't know how, but they didn't manage to land a single flaming firework on Trev. Today it's the kind of shit that would get reported to Worksafe, but back then it seemed to be a laugh. This was the environment I grew up a part of, where danger and fun went hand in hand.

Uncle Kim was tough like Grandad but had a cooler head than Dad. He was a talented boxer and could be intimidating if you were on his wrong side, but he was well-liked by the staff of the nursery. Kim was more reflective than Dad and is someone I continue to talk with today when I need to check if I am doing the right thing; he'll tell me directly if I am right or wrong and I have always trusted his judgement. Kim might be wise and respectful.

On the other side of the family were Nanna Jean, Mum's mum, and my step-grandfather Mike. Nanna Jean was and still is a very softly spoken lady and us kids would often stay with her and Mike when Mum and Dad went away. We loved to stir Nanna Jean up but even more fun was Mike, who was pranked constantly by the family.

Mike worked in sales for the nursery and would visit on Saturdays to check in with everybody. He loved the attention that came with being the target of the pranks. One day he arrived complaining of an upset stomach from a hot curry he'd had the night before and crawled into the toilet. Kim and Dad were never ones for sympathy and they loved an audience, so with workers all around the dispatch shed and a vulnerable target they couldn't resist the opportunity for chaos. Kim found a roll of 10,000 firecrackers, the kind you might see going off in a street on Chinese New Year. You wouldn't think a man of Kim's size could be stealthy but he was like a ninja as he crept towards the toilet door, with Dad behind him ready to light the crackers. Kim opened the door and Dad threw the roll of crackers in, then quickly pushed it closed before Mike even knew what was happening. "You bastard!" Mike shouted as the crackers started exploding in the tiny room. Kim held his body against the door to stop Mike from getting out and the shed sounded like a war zone for a solid two minutes. I watched this through tears of laughter, thinking it was the greatest prank I had ever seen. When the crackers finally went silent, Kim let the door open and the smoke poured out, revealing Mike sitting on the toilet, pants around his ankles and covered in red cracker paper.

I was an easily influenced child and I imitated my family's shenanigans from a young age; even today I still can't resist a good prank if the opportunity should arise. Mike was one of my favourite targets for my first pranks because he didn't take it too seriously; he enjoyed putting on a show when he discovered somebody was messing with him. With Dad or Kim I could only get away with so much, but I spent much of my youth and beyond thinking of ways to antagonise my step-grandfather. I started innocently as a child, hiding behind his couch with the TV remote and changing channels while he was trying to watch his shows. "There's something wrong with the TV again!" he yelled out to Nanna Jean.

When I was older, Mike took me out shooting rabbits in the nursery. I had a small air rifle to use and I had a bunny in my sights, but as I took the shot Mike happened to pass between the rabbit and I. The pellet hit his leg and he lost hit shit with me for pulling the trigger. I don't blame him, those pellets really hurt.

Mike did get some revenge on me eventually. My childhood bedroom had a wall of cabinetry with a massive stereo installed. The power for the stereo was wired in through the wall, so turning it on or off was difficult. Mike and Nanna Jean looked after my family's house when we went on holidays, and I thought it would be extremely funny to set the alarm on the stereo to come on at 3am every day, playing Metallica's Fuel at full volume. Nanna called Mum's phone after the first day and I rushed to answer, telling her Mum was busy because I knew she wanted to talk about the stereo. On the fifth day of our holiday, the same call arrived but Nanna had something different to tell me. "Benjamin, Mike has ripped the stereo out of the wall. He couldn't deal with the horrid music," she said. I no longer had my boom box, and I found out some pranks do have a price.

My sense of humour was moulded by my family and the older I got, the more I enjoyed playing a role in Dad and Uncle Kim's more risqué mischief. They bought Mike an obese blow-up doll as a joke birthday gift, which would have been funny enough on its own, until I suggested we rub Thai ornamental chillies over it. We grew the chillies at the nursery and they were so hot we needed to use gloves just to handle them. We inflated the doll and wiped the chillies over several parts (you can probably guess where), then rode to Mike's house on the property and left the doll next to his front door, knocking and running away. We stayed hidden at the side of the house and waited for him to come outside. He ventured out and laughed at the doll then returned inside, taking the doll with him. We stifled our laughter and crept to an open bedroom window, where we heard a sound similar to putting pool floaties on a kid, like skin against PVC. Through a gap in the curtains we could see Mike climbing on to the doll, making moaning sounds. He knew we were watching from somewhere and put on a show for us, really hamming it up. "We can fucking hear you, you sick cunt!" Kim yelled. It was a funny joke we thought and we were already moving on to the next idea, but an hour later we had a call from my dear old Nanna.

"Oh Benjamin, that was such a great prank, but why did you spray the whole doll with chilli? Mike's fingers are burning."

"I only put it around the holes, Nanna," I said.

Nanna paused as she pondered the new information. "You guys are so naughty, he has stuck his 'you know what' in the 'you know where'."

A couple of days later the doll was found deflated and sitting on Mike's fence. I promise he loved the attention, maybe just too literally this time.

The pranks rarely got me into serious trouble with the family, but one time stands out in my memory. I was hanging out with Mike and I had some little firecrackers, so I asked if I could throw one in the fireplace to see see what it would do, knowing full well it would likely blow red-hot coals out of the flames.

"Don't you dare, it will blow the fireplace apart," Mike said.

We were having corn on the cob with dinner and when I finished eating I went to throw the cob into the fire. I had the firecracker in my hand and as I threw the corn cob into the flames the cracker went too. Believe me when I say I never meant to throw the cracker in, because I knew it would do some damage. My hands scrambled into the fireplace to retrieve the cracker and luckily it didn't find the flames, but as I was trying to get it out Mike saw me messing with the fire and he thought I was trying to push the cracker in. I had never seen him so angry as he chased me around the house in a genuine fury. I escaped out the front door laughing, but I realised if he caught me he was going to have a pretty decent go. Outside the house, my uncle David was opening the gate to visit.

"Benny, look what I've just bought!" In his arms he had a bundle of fireworks. David's timing could not have been worse as Mike came charging out of the house, seeing the new crackers.

"You little bastard, if I catch up with you I will throttle you," he yelled. Nanna Jean had to calm Mike down and I stayed well out of his way for a time. I apologised and said it was stupid for me to be holding the cracker in the first place. The next day Mike told Dad what happened and he went mad and kicked me out of home. It turned into a real shit fight, which was so strange because it was a prank I had neither intended or completed. Uncle Kim stuck up for me as always, because he knew who I was. They were wild boys and so was I.

My extended family had an extended cast of interesting people who had lasting effects on my character. My Uncle Phil is Mum's brother and he was a joker as well, though more subtle than Dad and Uncle Kim. Our relationship grew as I got older because we had a lot of interests in common. Uncle Phil was renowned for his witty comments and enjoyed being the clever smart-ass, as did I. He also loved to do burnouts and I joined him in cars on many occasions to smoke some tyres to oblivion.

Alongside relatives, we also had very close friends who worked at the nursery and became part of our social lives. Brad was one of Dad's best friends in high school and was the acting manager at the nursery when the family was away. I looked up to him and he was a very respectable guy. His sons were close to my age and our families spent a lot of time together.

I had another unofficial uncle and auntie in Exmouth, where my family took holidays. Steve and Traci were very good friends

The family worked hard and played hard. Fishing holidays in Exmouth made some of my best memories.

of the family and Steve was a massive influence on my life. He owned a charter business called Blue Horizon and some of my best memories as a kid were going fishing with him. He always let me join him on the boat and we caught some monstrous fish together. I learned a lot about being a smart-ass from Steve, like when I asked him how deep the ocean was and he said, "Walk off the back of the boat and find out." I didn't know how to respond to answers like that at the time but I learned.

Steve was a great man, but not a skilled rider. I let him ride a brand new quad one day and he absolutely flew down the driveway for a test lap. He survived, so I told him to really give it some and he raced away once more but crashed into a row of ginger plants Dad had planted, ditching the quad and breaking his shoulder. Everything on the quad was bent and scratched and Steve was no better as we loaded him into the Landcruiser and took him to hospital.

Steve passed away about a year ago from a fall and a subsequent blood clot on the brain and I miss him dearly.

Then there was Uncle Russy. When I left school I took on more work at the nursery and Russy was often my partner in crime for the odd jobs we were given by Dad. One of the most dangerous and irritating tasks we had to do together was to whitewash the glasshouses. Twice a year we had to spray them with Parasylene to control the heat inside and it took two days to cover the lot. The glasshouse was 4.5-metres high and the only part to walk on was a 20-centimetre strip of steel guttering. I had to lift Russy up inside a crate using a tractor and then feed him the spraying hose while he navigated the narrow gutter, where it was all too easy to fall through the glass. I would hold the hose a bit too long on purpose to make him stumble and listen to him curse. Working safely was a skill I acquired later in life.

Even innocuous jobs sometimes became an ordeal with Russy, like driving to Exmouth to get the family's boat. It was a seriously big machine and we needed to take a truck up north to tow it. Russy and I hooked up the boat and started driving home but then we saw smoke pouring from the trailer, like it was doing a burnout. Sometime before we made the drive, one of Dad's friends had used the boat trailer and hit some pylons. Unknown to us, the crash had moved all the axles so they weren't perfectly in line with the trailer, and it was not noticeable until the boat was loaded on.

We pulled off the road and saw a rim had torn right off the trailer. We fixed the problem, putting it down to bad luck, and started again, but we didn't get too far before we had another blowout. The rims were snapping off at the axle because the metal was getting so hot. Tyre after tyre was being chewed up

The family boat 9-Lives.

and spat out almost every few minutes. We watched in disbelief on blowout number five when a rim flew off the trailer and bounced past the cabin of the truck. Russy pulled over into a filthy truck bay next to the road, downing a Coopers Red beer as he surveyed the damage. The truck bay was covered in old toilet paper and stains, and Russy had to lie down in the mess to change the tyre. "I'm over this shit," he said, his trademark line.

Russy loved cars and bikes and he performed spectacular wheelies past our family's house, which provided much of the inspiration for my own stunts later in life. That was until one day he fell off his bike on to bitumen and cut up his back and legs, right up to his bum. I still remember seeing all the road rash on his skin and thinking to myself how much it would hurt to fall off a bike badly. Good thing that was never going to happen to me, right?

Young Blood

My first visit to hospital came when I was a four-year-old and was surprisingly unrelated to any kind of vehicle or high speed crash. We had a pet doberman called Nero and I was obsessed with his furry ears. I sat next to him and twisted and pulled his ears around, I even tapped on his head with a shovel. The dog had enough of my constant harassment one day and understandably bit me on the back of the head. Shocked at Nero's snap, I covered my head with my hand and I returned to the house where Mum and Dad asked what happened. I knew I would be in trouble if I told them I was annoying the dog. "I fell on the rocks," I offered.

We took a family trip to the hospital so I could be stitched up, in what was the first of my many experiences with the Western Australian health system. Like many young children I must have been a slow learner, as a week later I was antagonising the dog again and grasping those irresistible fuzzy ears. As if he hadn't been clear on the message last time, he gave me another nip to the head. I was not sure if my parents believed me or not as I provided the same flimsy excuse a second time for my bleeding skull. I'm certain they must have been skeptical by this stage.

We returned to the hospital, where the response from the medical staff took on a more serious tone. The repeated injuries made the staff suspicious of child abuse and they interrogated my parents, questioning how one child could be so accident prone. They're still asking the same question in my thirties of course.

My next visit to hospital came near Christmas one year. I had discovered a trove of presents hidden in the house and I wanted to show my sister Jodi. I ran to get her but I heard someone coming, so to avoid getting caught in the act I cleared out of the room and jumped over a lounge chair, painfully splitting my head open on the corner edge of a wall.

I was nine years old when I finally had my first accident on wheels, and it was a big one. I was riding a Badger quad beside a fence and the road ended in a blind T-junction. As I reached the intersection I collided with my sister, who was riding from the other direction and was just as surprised as I was. I T-boned the side of her bike and I remember feeling like I was in a tumble dryer as I sailed through the air and hit the ground. The impact knocked me out for a short time and I woke up to the horror of a badly injured thigh, cut open and bleeding. The flaps of skin left hanging against the wound terrified me and I started screaming, knowing I was hurt but also knowing I was going to be in trouble. Dad heard the crash from 200 metres away and raced to the accident scene, where he wrapped my leg in a towel and took me to hospital once more.

My injuries were a result of bravado and childish stupidity at times, but bad luck also played a role. When I was in sixth grade I stepped on a tree stump and sliced my right foot open. Most kids would have escaped with a splinter, but not me.

Not long afterwards I got into a fight at school. A kid was picking on me, so I punched him in the head, breaking my fingers and hand and resulting in my first experience with getting pins inserted to hold my cracked bones in place. Little did I realise it would be far from my last.

As I grew older, I was introduced to more possibilities for trouble and carnage. One of my favourite things to mess with at the nursery was the boiler, which protected the plants from the cold by heating water that ran through the glasshouses. Coal was fed into a centre furnace to heat the pipes and I loved screwing around with it because it had fire, and anything destructive had my attention when I was younger – it still does I admit.

I was 14, and my brother Luke was enjoying his birthday party. Dad told me to put the wrapping paper from Luke's gifts into the furnace, a job I enjoyed. The coals were still hot, and I eagerly expected a good flame from the paper, so I stuffed the colourful wrapping inside and was disappointed when it did not catch alight after hoping to see it burn instantaneously. I had to accelerate the process, so I went to a petrol bowser we had on site and filled a mop bucket with fuel. I happily returned to the furnace and poured the accelerant in, but still got nothing. Figuring the coals did not have enough heat to light the paper or the fuel, I leaned through the doors to light it by hand, right as the petrol reached some of the red-hot coals at the bottom of the furnace and ignited.

I was blown from my feet by the force of the explosion and my face caught much of the flame. As I realised what happened I looked around and the conifers around the boiler were set ablaze, as was the wrapping paper – safe to say. I feared a hiding from Dad and ran to get to the nursery's fire fighting unit, which sat on a trailer and was towed by a quad. Thankfully the tank was filled with water as I climbed on board to hurry back to the fire. I wound on the throttle, and then my heart dropped as the motor began to sputter. It was out of fuel! I frantically disconnected the trailer and ran to find another quad to use. I finally found one and returned to the inferno to douse the flames, then did my best to clean up the charred area before running home to our bathroom, being careful not to draw the attention of my parents. I stared into the mirror and noticed my skin was already red and blistering and my eyebrows were singed. I wasn't in much pain and I thought maybe I could shave off the hair so no one could tell it had been burned; I was only worried about the trouble I was going to be in. My absence lasted long enough for Mum to come looking for me and when she found me in the bathroom I spilled the beans. "I buggered up, Mum. I got burned. It will be alright but."

Mum put me into a cold bath and I noticed my arm had started to go light blue in colour. That was when the pain started. It hit me all over my body like I had just been smacked on the ass and I screamed out from the self-inflicted torture. Mum piled me into her brand new Holden Clubsport and we took off to hospital, reaching speeds over 130kph. We know this for a fact because she got a ticket from a speed camera on South Street.

After the doctors stabilised me I was taken to Princess Margaret Hospital, the primary children's hospital in Perth, and I had to endure the skin peeling from my arms and face over the following weeks. I've had a lot of painful experiences since, but I will never forget the pain of those burns.

Pain is supposed to be a good teacher, but not for me. I was 17 and we were doing demolition at the nursery before it shifted locations. I was having a good time knocking buildings down and tearing the place up. I wasn't old enough to drink yet, but the Balinese workers my family employed secretly gave me beers and we would run amuck. The old buildings sat on concrete pads, where we did burnouts, and because the area around the nursery was not developed there was no one around to bother us.

I had my friends come over for some drinks and a bonfire and I thought I was the biggest legend out, like most teenagers. Dad said we could rip out any remaining trees or plants to stack together for the bonfire because it would save him time. We piled anything that would burn into a stack and once again I thought petrol was a great idea to accelerate the flames. Drunk and not paying attention, I wandered too close and when I lit the petrol I was caught in the flash, sustaining second degree burns. I was back at hospital for a seventh time and I wasn't even 18.

You could call me accident prone, but it was a consequence of an inquisitive mind and the fearless nature I inherited from the people around me.

Growth

In 1994, Grandad was diagnosed with cancer and he passed away on January 22, 1995 at 60 years old. Dad and Uncle Kim took over the reins of the nursery and built on the foundation Grandad had laid. Dad explained to me when I was younger that he was the businessman – he procured all the new business for the nursery and was the one that made the money. Uncle Kim was the one who put the strategy into action with all of the workers, and was more hands on. Nanna stayed in the office doing the bookwork. Dad raised me to think he was the one with the smarts, and a visionary for the business.

At the nursery's peak the numbers were impressive. The family business potted and planted 20,000 poinsettias a year and all were pre-sold. Contracts were in place with hardware chain Bunnings and at one stage Canning Plant Farm was their main supplier, with anywhere from $200,000 to $400,000 worth of plants a month going into their stores across Australia. Hulking semi trucks arrived at the nursery to take full loads across the country to the east coast, and their arrival required all hands on deck to fulfil the orders. Big department stores like Big W, Kmart and Target each had their own garden centres too and Canning Plant Farm was there to supply them. The nursery's size varied from 30 to 50 employees, peaking during the Christmas season. That time of year was always busy, as were school holidays, and it wasn't unusual for the family to do well over half a million dollars of plant sales in December. Uncle Kim reckons the biggest single day ever at the nursery saw 25,500 two litre pots sent out, while another time 15,500 of the big five litre pots went out the door.

The nursery grew 40,000 hydrangeas alone. Chrysanthemums, zygocactus, kalanchoe, African violets, golden pencil pines, bookleafs, hanging baskets, mini gardens, Christmas trees – the list went on. Propagation alone required Dad, Kim, Brad and Russy to spend hours before sunrise each morning making cuttings. From 7am to 10am they moved on to weeding, then they took morning tea before attending to other odd jobs for what was left of the day.

After Grandad passed away, Dad and Kim implemented new ideas to expand the nursery's customer base. Instead of being a purely wholesale supplier to other nurseries, they opened up a trade centre that was like a supermarket for plants and landscaping supplies. It was called Trademart, and they even allowed other wholesale nurseries to bring their plants in; it became a one stop shop for landscaping businesses. Uncle Kim was never a fan but it was Dad's baby and to his credit the plan worked.

I learned much at the nursery when I was growing up, but I was in people's way a lot too. I was a smart talking young fella, taking after the male role models around me. I loved to stir up the staff and the Balinese workers at the nursery were my favourite audience. A lot of Balinese workers were employed there, many of whom became very good family friends (before the Balinese, Grandad had Dutch workers). They were immigrants to Australia who arrived with a strong work ethic and were making a life for themselves in Perth. As I grew older and started learning about how business works, I could appreciate these men and their work ethic; they were a strong foundation for the nursery. The nursery started with one man from Bali, Anton, and each year he was able to introduce a couple more friends or family who were keen to work.

When I was younger, I heard one of the Bali boys being teased as 'Johnny Bucktooth Buzzard', because of his massive front teeth. I was a smart-ass in training and repeated the insult to him, but I wasn't quick enough to get away in time, so Johnny grabbed me and put sand down my jocks to teach me a lesson. There were consequences for my fun!

Chief (also called Bagus, handsome in Indonesian) was the oldest one out of the Balinese group, and he would stay very quiet until I revved him up. I was slightly older and we were digging trees out with an excavator, so I gave him a bit of a nudge with the excavator bucket and knocked him into a hole. He really fired up and threw a shovel at me, and then started hanging off the end of the bucket yelling at me while I was swinging around in a circle. Fortunately the Balinese workers never kept a grudge as I pushed the boundaries of messing with them.

Further growth for the nursery meant more space was needed and as the Perth metropolitan area expanded, Canning Vale was becoming rapidly urbanised. The bushland around the nursery was developed and the land rose in value. There had been a rough plan to eventually move to Serpentine, south east of Perth, where land was cheap enough to purchase in large lots but remained within an hour's drive of Perth. Grandad already had land out there where he enjoyed running his cattle, but he wasn't supportive of moving the nursery when he was alive. Dad wanted to move to Serpentine and build a new house, while Kim would have preferred to wait a few more years.

Canning Vale was a prime location for the nursery and it produced efficiently. Forty years of growing meant all the kinks had been resolved and production ran like clockwork. The nursery was sectioned into corridors, each with 15 beds of plants that were 150 metres long by 1.8 metres wide. Fences separated each section and the spatial organisation allowed weeding to be performed methodically. Family homes on site meant somebody was there 24 hours a day in case of a failure. Irrigation systems, pumps, controllers and liquid feed were all susceptible to breakdowns or human error, but with someone from the family always close by, the damage was kept to a minimum.

Because the Trademart was located on the property, replacing stock was a simple process; the plants were literally being grown right outside the back door. Two or three workers could keep the centre stocked with Canning Plant Farm's quality plants, even at the busiest times.

Dad and Kim were ambitious and the move to Serpentine was irresistible – it was planned to be just like Canning Vale, only bigger. On my birthday in 2001, Dad and I went for a drive to Serpentine to scope out some land and we found a 50 acre block on Karnup Road that was perfect. It was an old vegetable farm on flat terrain, already equipped with a dam, farm house and shed. The groundwater was reliable and high quality. Dad called Uncle Kim to come and take a look at the property, and the pair of them began inquiries. Negotiations took place in cloak and dagger style, with Dad and Kim disguising their past and intentions because they expected the owner to be stubborn on pricing if he found out who they were. They secured the property and the massive operation to shift Canning

Plant Farm's well-established operation had begun.

The Serpentine nursery was built with the latest and greatest technology from around the world and it was planned meticulously. Dad and Kim travelled to Germany to purchase new potting machines, allowing production to be ramped up. The glasshouse was sourced from Holland and was built from actual glass instead of the fibreglass used in Canning Vale. Spanning four acres in size, it was easily one of the largest in Western Australia. Inside were oil burners to keep the temperature consistent, no matter the weather. The irrigation featured redundant systems so the dam could be used as a back up, and the groundwater – low in iron – was better than Canning Vale.

The move to Serpentine came when I was getting old enough to take a more active role in the business. I never said a great deal about what I was learning, but I watched and took everything in. During school holidays I spent my time at the nursery, sometimes working, sometimes just being a pain in the ass. I started from the bottom of the ladder, taking pots off the conveyor belt and putting them on to a trailer. Dad later let me pot my own plants, giving me a dollar a plant. On weekends I could plant 1000 of the things by myself, so it was a pretty lucrative deal as a young lad. While other kids were mucking around with BMX bikes and having a blast on their holidays, I was potting plants and learning about weed control. I was taught how to mix soils and use liquid feed, studied grow rates and gained more knowledge about running a wholesale nursery. My interest depended on how I was getting on with Dad at the time; frequent clashes as I grew older often made it hard to be at the nursery.

In the early days of Serpentine the plan worked well. The sale of Canning Vale provided fresh cash reserves and Serpentine looked set to provide an even greater return in years to come.

On Wheels

Freestyle motocross was my first love in extreme sports and I was doing stunts before I could read. The move to the new nursery provided more room for plants, but also space to explore my growing love for doing stupid things on motorbikes.

I was given my first quad when I was five years old. It was a tiny Suzuki four wheeler with a 50cc motor and a single gear. Even at such a young age I was disappointed with how slow the quad was as I searched for more throttle, but I learned all of my early riding lessons on that Suzuki. Dad cut me a track with his loader and most days after school I could be found flying around there, or annoying the nursery workers as I rode around making a nuisance of myself.

We had a shallow concrete pond in front of our house, maybe six inches deep, where I performed my first stunts as a young fella. I rode in like a demon and spun the wheels on the algae, splashing up the water. After that I hooned to the dispatch shed, where I would watch the trucks reverse up and lift their hydraulic tail gates. I balanced the quad on two wheels and rode underneath those tail gates for a thrill, thinking I was Evel Knievel. That poor quad was punished and eventually it blew up, bringing a merciful end to its life.

I stuck to riding inside the nursery when I was younger, because the area outside the boundaries could be rough. Only three houses were nearby, and one of them was regularly causing trouble. Sirens always seemed to be on the way – police cars, fire engines, ambulances, or some combination of the three – and this amused me greatly as a kid, as I didn't yet understand the consequences. For my family it was more concerning.

One day the family from the bad house came to Mum and Dad's place in the corner of the nursery, and asked Mum and Aunt Hilary for money. When they were told to go away, they threatened to kill the girls. The Stevens men later went down the road to sort the situation out. They were hard blokes and I guess the message got across.

It was a truly miserable and wretched place. Someone from the house once had a drug overdose and was left lying dead in a ditch outside. The poor man's family didn't even do anything about it. The end came when a fire started at the house, and the story I heard was that the firefighters stood back and let it burn, because they had been falsely called out there so many times. Grandad bought the land and turned it into a tip, which was a better result for the whole street.

I saved up pocket money for my next ride, mowing lawns and doing jobs for Dad. We traded the little Suzuki in and bought a Badger, an 80cc quad. This one had some more grunt and also took much abuse from me. I would get into the concrete pond and go stupid, clicking it into third gear and doing as many donuts as I could, treating the water feature like a skate bowl. I had a small jump built for me on the motorbike track and I charged at it as fast I could, hitting maybe 50kph. This quad was really the first one my friends and I could get in trouble on. As well as the crash with my sister I mentioned earlier, it also threw my buddy Mitch off over some ripples, breaking his arm. It seemed unbreakable, until on a flying speed run one day I hit a jump and snapped all of the wheels off at the axles.

Strangely enough, that wasn't the end for the Badger. Last year I went to my friend Travis' house and saw he had a Badger too. I took a closer look and noticed a significant mark on the guard where one of my friends had hit a trailer – this was the same quad! I couldn't believe the old girl was still surviving.

The next machine to arrive was a Honda XR80, the first two wheeler I owned. It was a Christmas present and lasted only five days at my hands. My friend Shane had a motorbike track at his place with bigger jumps, and I went around there to have a go. I was keen to start riding and didn't put my motocross boots on. I was blasting around a corner when a well cover caught my leg, splitting my shin open. I had another trip to hospital (number eight of my life, for those counting) to be stitched up and the next day the bike was stolen from our house. Maybe it just wasn't meant to be.

I was without a bike while I saved my money and then upgraded to a Honda XR100. These bikes aren't supposed to die, but few get to meet a rider like me and I punished that poor machine. This was the first bike I could do real burnouts on and I went through many back tyres just from smoking it up. The movie Mad Max featured a stunt where one of the bikies does a perfect circle donut with a line through the middle; I always tried to copy that.

I returned to four wheels when I got my first quad racer, a Honda TRX400. That was the first time I had excess horsepower to use and the motor was mounted close to the rear of the chassis, which meant I could wheelstand everywhere. I had proper power and I loved it. At the time we were starting to build the new nursery, so whenever the family went there I could take the quad and ride the wheels off it. We had a big Caterpillar loader on the property and when Uncle Kim wasn't busy he pushed dirt to make jumps for me. That was my first experience with big air, where I had time to feel the quad flying and could balance it out for the landing – the basic elements of freestyling.

The TRX400 met its end in Canning Vale. We were still finishing demolishing the nursery when Russy offered me my first beer, a Coopers Red. I wasn't really into beer, but I had one and became drunk very quickly. I rode the quad to the back of the nursery and smoked the rear tyres until the motor cried enough.

I was never excited by the idea of racing my quads or bikes, which was surprising looking back because I had a very competitive personality. Instead I found an outlet in boxing. Uncle Kim was a very good boxer back in his day and his former coach had started a boxing gym in Maddington, so I went there for a look and started to get into training. I wasn't into physical sports much, and I wasn't the best boxer, but I enjoyed the activity and made good friends at the gym.

Boxing ended up consuming a lot of my life through Year 12 and I trained up to four nights a week, sometimes more if I was getting ready for a fight. My trainer Rory was a legend of a man, a really good guy who was another role model for my life. He did a lot for me, taking me under his wing and teaching me to be a good, respectable fighter. Boxing interrupted my schooling because all I wanted to do was train and be as fit as possible.

Growing up I was shit scared of Dad, because if I stepped out of line he would be on to me hard. I was never suspended from school because I knew I would cop a hiding at home. When I began boxing I started gaining more confidence and took less crap from Dad. My life became busier when I finished school and I earned my driver's licence, and boxing found less of a place in my late teens, but I still had enough time for getting off road.

I had a brand new Raptor 660 next. It didn't last long before the engine blew up in a mess of crank, pistons and rods, and I traded it in for a Bombardier 650. This quad was built by Can-Am and was meant to be the quickest and fastest of all time. It could really move and did great powerskids. We took it to the Canning Vale sand dunes where a mate went flying over the top of one of the hills and hit a fence, destroying the quad. He paid to fix it all but I sold it afterwards, not wanting anything to do with a crashed and repaired machine.

I went back to two wheels with a Yamaha YZ450. This was when I first really started to push my skills in freestyle. I created a compound to ride in at the nursery, using the earthmoving machines whenever they were available. My friends and I created a playground of jumps, tabletops, berms and canyons in a space where we didn't have to annoy anyone and could just focus on riding. I loved the feeling of soaring through the air or spraying dirt through a corner.

My good mates came to ride with me, but when I built the compound it was also my first experience with a different type of person, the type who will use someone and move on. A few of these people became friends just so they could ride at the property. Young and naïve, I thought I was Mr Popular and as far as I was concerned, the more the merrier. These people never helped to take care of the compound and didn't show appreciation for the place, but I hadn't experienced that behaviour before and didn't know how to recognise it.

I liked riding where I could control the environment, especially after I had my first decent accident at the Canning Vale sand dunes in 2004. I made a stupid decision and didn't inspect the area first, and went flying over the top of a dune on to a road where someone had dumped a load of sand and rubble. I didn't see the pile until too late and I came crashing down, hearing my left knee crack. I was lying in the dust for an hour yelling out for help, until one of my friends finally found me crippled on the ground. I went to hospital where I needed an operation on my knee.

I knew that riding bikes meant crashing but that was the first really bad one that took me off my feet for a while, and it made me acknowledge the risks. Of course, plenty more were to come.

Life at High Speed

The Stevens family were revheads with plenty of cash to burn and if there is one motorsport perfectly suited for that, it's drag racing. It's an extremely simple sport at heart, two cars or bikes and a straight line of track, but some serious time and money can be spent at the professional levels.

Watching drag racing was one of our favourite family activities. We'd drive to Ravenswood Raceway, near Mandurah in Western Australia, and watch the racing all night. A lot of veteran drag racers still talk about Ravenswood with fondness for its after-race party atmosphere, but I wasn't old enough to appreciate it at the time.

Victor Bray was a legend in Australian drag racing (he still is) and whenever we heard he was coming to town we made sure we were there. Uncle Phil was a member of Victor's pit crew, as well as a few other teams, so we could take photos of us sitting in the cars and meet the drivers behind the scenes. We'd also go to the track on Boxing Day each year to watch the Nitro Funny Cars and celebrate my birthday.

The Ravenswood track closed in 2000 and drag racing moved to a new venue, Perth Motorplex. The Motorplex was much closer to Perth and the easier journey meant we attended more events. Uncle Phil organised for me to do some work experience with a race workshop called Street Quick Performance and the owner, John Lloyd, arranged for me to be on the pit crew for a racer called Dave Simpson. I jumped at the idea and loved being involved with a team. Dave drove a Top Doorslammer, the same type of car as Victor Bray, and I became addicted to the power of the machines. Dave even let me sit in the car while they warmed up the engine to give me a sense of the horsepower I was working on.

Phil was friends with Greg Gower, a talented drag racing engine tuner, and Greg's wife was a travel agent who organised holidays for Brett Stevens (no relation), one of Australia's most well known drag racers at the time. Through this few degrees of separation, Dad and Uncle Kim got to know Brett. He was going to Bali and wanted a local guide, so Dad was asked if one of his Balinese workers from the nursery would be up for the job. Dad agreed, and as a drag racing fan he was hoping he would get to meet Brett in person at a later stage. One of the Bali workers, Wuyan, travelled with Brett to show him around the island, and when Brett came back to Perth he caught up with Dad and Kim.

In 2004, Brett was a great showman of drag racing, driving both a Top Doorslammer, and a nitro-fuelled Harley-Davidson in the Top Bike class. He had corporate sponsorship from Jack Daniel's and was a popular racer with fans. Brett was expanding his team, with plans to build and operate more cars and bikes. He said he could build Dad a Top Doorslammer, and Kim had always wanted to race a Nitro Harley. They were just fans and neither of them had raced anything truely powerful before, but they loved the idea and the vehicles went into production.

While Dad and Kim were waiting for these new toys to be

Dad (second from left) and I (third from left) get some lessons on maintaining a Top Doorslammer.

built, Brett asked us to join his team for some events so we would have some knowledge on how to maintain the car and bike when they were ready. I got to see all the ins and outs of a Top Doorslammer and was flown to Brisbane and Sydney to help crew on his existing teams. My jobs ranged from helping out on the engine side to being the kid who could work a video camera. The way Brett ran his team was highly professional and his pit crew weren't at events to party, they were there to race. Brett had a wild reputation, but the whole team were well behaved for the most part. Anyone who stepped out of line had Brett to answer to, and he didn't take any shit.

Soon Dad's car was ready and we flew to Willowbank Raceway in Queensland for a private test where he could get his drag racing licence. The car was beautiful, a late model Holden Monaro with lightning airbrushed all over the body. It had an aluminium racing engine over eight litres in size, topped off with a giant supercharger and making about 2500 horsepower. Dad's Monaro had the same parts as Brett's own race cars and the capability to be just as fast. Dad had been in hot cars before, but the experience of a Top Doorslammer was very different. I will never forget the look on his face when we started the car up for the first time with him in the driver's seat – I think he needed a change of pants.

To be fair, not many people know what to expect when they are new to drag racing and I think he imagined a loud street car. A Top Doorslammer looks something like an ordinary car from the outside, but it is really just a very powerful engine and a bunch of tubes welded together to keep the driver safe. The whole thing shakes and rumbles, the fumes from the methanol fuel burn the eyes of anyone standing too close and the noise of the exhaust drowns out voices easily – it can be very intimidating. On the first day of testing we started with just burnouts as Dad learned how to drive. I'm not sure he even launched it for a run on that first day, but his confidence soon grew and he started to drive the beast further and further down the track.

Dad's name didn't appear on any record books and there weren't many trophies but he was having a ball going racing. The deal with Brett was 'fly in and drive', which suited Dad perfectly. We turned up as a team and Brett had the car serviced and ready to go. At the end of an event we packed everything away and flew out, leaving any repairs and maintenance to the team at his Queensland workshop.

Looking back, drag racing was the closest I had to a healthy father and son relationship, bonding through our mutual interest in the sport. Dad was hard on me growing up and I resented him for the treatment he handed out. On race day though, we had to trust each other. He relied on me to make sure he was safe in the car and I relied on him to drive well after our hard work. I was an important part of the team and if Dad became aggressive with me while we were racing I could tell him to piss off. He needed his pit crew and without us he wouldn't be racing.

They were good days. We were all friends on the race team and every event we attended became a party and an adventure. I shared a room with Anthony Begley for most events. These days Begs drives a Top Fuel dragster and runs a very professional garage door business, but he was one of us wild boys on the road. We got stuck into each other fighting, we'd shake up beers and spray them around, and one time I filled a pillow full of water and belted Begs right over the back as he was unpacking his bag. By the end of three days at a race event our hotel room would be trashed, like a touring rock band had been through there. Brett had to give us some stern talks. He insisted on running the team professionally and here we were on the border of throwing televisions out the window.

Sometimes Brett dished it out though. After my knee operation from the Canning Vale crash I was on crutches, but I still wanted to work on the car. While I was concentrating hard on clutch maintenance, Brett took the crutches and sawed them in half, then taped them together with transparent tape so it looked as if they were still whole. I finished working on the clutch and picked up the crutches, but as soon as I put my weight on them they collapsed and I fell to the ground, much to the amusement of the rest of the crew. I'm glad someone had a laugh out of it.

After racing we would all go out and get drunk, and the biggest parties came when the events were rained out. The craziest I can remember was in Sydney where we ended up at the casino and ran amuck. We were kicked out for being too rowdy and I started a wrestling match with Begs right outside the front door, tripping him and sending him falling down the stairs. Security had to move us on and we were still scrapping when we got to our car. We weren't being aggressive, just play fighting, but it was getting pretty rough and one of our crew guys, Chris Mills (another drag racing legend), put his hand on my knee and told us to settle down. I was drunk and having a great time so I grabbed his finger and twisted it to annoy him, only to break it. The next time we went racing he still had a splint on his finger and I had to spend a lot of time apologising.

To compete on race day in the Top Doorslammer class, Dad first had to qualify into a field of the quickest eight cars. Often we didn't qualify quick enough, so we had an extra day

Working together on a drag racing team helped my relationship with Dad initially, we had to trust each other.

to drink. We couldn't even help with Kim; he didn't want us around his bike after we had been drinking. He approached his racing more maturely because he stood a chance of winning events and competing for a championship.

Dad and Kim raced as part of Brett's stable for a couple of seasons before they decided to branch out on their own. The fly in, fly out deal was convenient but expensive. They purchased a semi-trailer to transport the team and we started racing more locally in Perth. This allowed me to get more involved as we now had to take care of maintenance between events. Racing at the Motorplex was more relaxing for everyone, despite the extra load of maintaining the cars. We had to replace broken or old parts, grind clutches and make sure the car was still safe. Getting to take this hot rod apart between events meant I knew it like the back of my hand.

Perhaps the most most generous thing Dad ever did for me was letting me make some passes to get my Australian National Drag Racing Association (ANDRA) licence. I hadn't driven anything faster than a Toyota Hilux on the track before, but working on his Monaro gave me familiarity. I had sat in the car during a bunch of engine warm ups over the years which helped me understand the controls and gave me some idea of what to expect. On my first launch I hit the transition beautifully (going from clutch to full throttle) and the Monaro got up and boogied. I'd never felt anything so fast before, and every single time I went back on to the track during the day I progressed more, making the burnouts longer on each pass. It was really good fun to drive and I enjoyed all that power at my right foot. But the Monaro didn't frighten the living daylights out of me and I thought I'd need something more extreme later on if I was going to keep drag racing.

ANDRA officials signed me off on each stage, letting me go further and further down the track until I was allowed to make a full quarter mile pass. I prepared for the final licensing stage mentally, ready to experience the top speed of the car. I smashed the throttle pedal and did not let it up, focused on achieving my goal. The giant rear tyres gripped and the car shoved me back in the seat under acceleration, the supercharged motor singing to the top of each gear. The environment around me blurred with speed, but I was in total control. I crossed the finish line at 305kph and threw a lever to release the parachutes, waiting to feel the 'hit', but there was nothing.

I realised the car was not slowing down. I hauled on the brakes but I could already see the end of the braking area coming up real fast. The drag strip at Perth Motorplex has 600 metres of bitumen to brake on, followed by a sand trap and

Getting to drive the Top Doorslammer was a highlight, and gave me a sense of the speeds possible in drag racing.

finally a catch net. As the distance started running out I started shitting myself, because I had seen how the sand could tear up the body of the car and get into the engine, and I really didn't want to leave it damaged. Out of room and out of options I locked up the brakes, spun the steering wheel to the left, popped the clutch for some engine braking and brought the car to a screeching halt. The parachutes limply dropped out as I turned off the engine and let my heart rate settle.

Okay, that one frightened me.

Warning Signs

Shortly after Dad and Kim started drag racing, Mum had to go into Armadale Hospital for a routine operation. The doctors performing the operation perforated her bowel in a case of gross negligence, and Mum nearly died. She was transferred to the intensive care unit of Murdoch Hospital and recovered over time, but the effects of the episode lingered long afterwards – they still do today. Mum's close call with death and her long period of recovery took Dad's attention away from the new nursery, which was only just getting on its feet.

Uncle Kim was left to run the business, doing the majority of the work by himself while Dad spent time with Mum in the hospital. The Canning Vale nursery required three experienced family members in charge to keep it running smoothly, but Serpentine was a much larger operation and Uncle Kim struggled with the workload.

Mum had a hard time getting her health back to normal. She started taking more prescription medications and it was at this time in my life things began to go a little haywire. Dad began to take medication of his own as he sought ways to cope with the pressures of Mum's near-death experience and the expansion of the nursery. His personality became more erratic and frustrating than before; the family didn't know if he was going to be the happiest man on Earth or the angriest from one day to the next, and he was already prone to a vicious temper.

My brother Luke, sister Jodi and I started noticing the inconsistencies in our home lives and around the nursery. The dream was for the family business to be passed on to a third generation, with myself and my cousin Brod, Uncle Kim's son, taking over. But the family began to feel divided and the business started to show some financial issues. At the nursery's height, the assets alone were worth $28 million – without even taking cashflow into consideration. Now the family was regretful about the timing of the Serpentine move because Perth property boomed shortly after the land at Canning Vale was sold; just holding on to the land for five more years might have seen them double the windfall.

Despite the planning that went into the new nursery, inherent problems with the site were proving difficult to solve. The quality of the indoor plants was not as good as Canning Vale even with the new glasshouses, which had a large amount of borrowed money hanging over them. Serpentine had no fences between sections, and the daily 'Fremantle Doctor' (an afternoon south-westerly wind Perth is famous for) blew straight through the nursery – some days it knocked the plants right over. The wind made weed control difficult and the unwanted plants proved almost impossible to keep in check. We could watch as dandelion seeds glided through the rows, infecting large parts of the nursery. The perfect conditions we supplied for our plants, with liquid feed and high quality soil, were just as perfect for the weeds and they germinated rapidly. One weed in a load of soil had the potential to infect a whole batch of plants. Weed control had been part of the culture at Canning Vale, with a team of employees spending three hours a day weeding sections. Maybe it was the scale of Serpentine or perhaps it was a lack of oversight, but that culture drifted away and the nursery suffered.

Dad's decisions for the nursery became hard to understand for the family. He wanted to pot thousands of plants of a variety that wasn't selling, and if he didn't get his way he became easily frustrated, often taking it out on Nanna Val. She looked after the accounts and was still an important part of the business, providing wise advice from her decades of experience.

Kim and I spoke about the need for fences within the boundaries of the nursery to try and stop the weeds, but Dad felt fences weren't needed and wanted an open plan. Dad and Kim were finding it more difficult to make decisions together, and my ideas were often discounted completely by Dad, even if they were helpful.

Despite the problems at the nursery, I was learning how to mix soils and spray for pests and generally increasing my cultivation knowledge. This side of the business interested me greatly, but then Dad put me in charge of the dispatch shed instead – a job he knew I hated. No matter how I had things organised, he always found something he wanted changed. The trailers would be parked wrong, or he wanted the trolleys in a different spot. The dispatch shed sapped my enthusiasm, as did Dad's vindictive nature towards me.

I saw myself running the nursery one day and despite our troubled relationship, I wanted to follow in Dad's footsteps in business. I strived to learn more about the industry and really put in some effort to address parts of the business where I could see a need for improvement, but his constant criticism for criticism's sake was exhausting. My personality doesn't allow me to give up when someone puts roadblocks in front of me, but there's a difference between battling the odds and taking on someone who was relentlessly trying to take me down a peg. I lost a lot of respect for Dad at the time and I felt forced away from him after all our good times drag racing, where we had felt like a father and son team. I thought back more to the hidings I copped when I was younger, where he went over the edge.

Dad had always been headstrong, but the erratic decisions were having more of an impact on the business. He never thought he was wrong and that made him hard to work for, both for our family and staff. He employed managers at the nursery who told him what needed to change, but he would disagree and tell them to go away, in less flattering terms.

We had a Taiwanese worker at the nursery who had a disagreement with one of my mates, which finished with a threat to cut my mate's throat. My friend Paul 'Plugger' Murdoch was at the nursery helping out and saw the argument, so he talked to Dad about it, concerned the threat may be realised. "You can't have your workers threatening to knife each other," Plugger said. Dad refused to listen and instead of taking action, he told Plugger to get his things and not to come back, because he didn't like being told what to do by someone lower on the ladder.

I still loved my days drag racing with Dad, but it became frustrating and worrying for the family to watch him drive. He was having a harder time keeping the car driving in a straight line and the risk was becoming more serious. He blamed the car for the handling issues and some people agreed, but Dad was also on a lot of prescription medications at the time. Brett Stevens and I discussed Dad's driving, and he said he had become distant with Dad. Brett noticed the effect of the medications not just on Dad's personality but also on his racing skills and was

The Top Doorslammer coming back after a run, showing the scars of an impact with the wall.

concerned for his safety, as was I.

At an event at Willowbank Raceway in Queensland he crashed into the wall next to the track really hard and I thought he might have been injured. The impact was hard enough to bend one of the rims and damage the rear end and suspension in the back of the car. The pit crew became disheartened as the car became more frequently sidelined by these troubles, after they put many hours of effort into maintenance behind the scenes. Some of Dad's mates started telling him it was time to get out of the seat and maybe give me a go. He didn't like hearing that anyone could do something better than him, but I am sure he realised there was a problem, whether it was caused by the equipment or not.

In 2008, Dad's drag racing career came to a close. Again the Monaro crashed into the safety barriers, this time in Perth, and damaged the whole left hand side of the body. The plan had been to let me do some more test runs the next day, so the team and I stayed up all night to repair the car and we had it ready to race again.

My turn in the car saw it launch well and it was on a really good pass until I noticed the engine was losing power and I released my foot from the throttle pedal, abandoning the run. On returning to the pits, we discovered one of the cylinders had a badly hurt piston and ring. This type of damage can come from a parts failure or a bad call on the tune up.

Afterwards, Dad told me it was my fault the engine was damaged, which stung me badly after we'd spent all night repairing the car from his crash. I wasn't responsible for the tune up, and the only way to cause serious damage to the motor from a driving perspective was to over rev it or stay in the throttle when it was showing obvious warning signs, like vibrations or a loss in power. We looked at the data logger, which recorded the motor's vital signs and my actions as a driver, and the graphs showed I couldn't have done anything differently.

I didn't know at the time, but that would be the last day I went drag racing with Dad's team. He planned to take a break from racing and do some upgrades to the car, but later he decided to sell. I don't think he had the motivation to drive again after the crash, and life's distractions were also mounting, between the nursery and Mum's health.

I was devastated when Dad sold the car, and even more when I found out he sold the engine for $20,000 and the chassis for another $20,000 – pennies on the dollar for the equipment. He was shafted big time by somebody in the drag racing community and while I can't mention names, I like to think Karma comes back for people who take advantage of others' state of mind.

Uncle Kim was more successful on his Nitro Harley. He had picked up the riding style straight away and was only getting better the more he rode. He won a number of events on the national tour and was a real contender to take out the whole ANDRA Top Bike series for a few years, with a best overall championship finish of third nationally. I was intrigued by how Kim's motorcycle worked, but it never had my full attention until Dad sold his car. Even though the performances of the family's race vehicles were comparable, they were two completely different concepts. The Harley had less maintenance to worry about, but it was more difficult to tune. It had only two cylinders and they needed to be perfect, fuelled by powerful yet fickle nitromethane.

Even though Dad gave up on racing, Kim kept going and he even got back into the fold with Brett Stevens for a while to race as part of a super-team. I still had a hunger to be part of the scene and I became more involved with Kim's racing. I thought Nitro Harleys were the second craziest thing you could do on two wheels, right after freestyle.

Freestyler

When I was working on the pit crew of Dad's drag car, he banned me from owning any more quads or bikes. He was trying to control my extreme side, worried I wasn't going to live until I was 21. "I'm still here, aren't I?" I boasted during my 21st birthday speech.

Not long after that, my girlfriend of the time convinced me to get back into quads, so I bought a new Yamaha Raptor 700. She bought a quad too so we could go out and ride trails together. I thought I was finished with freestyle, because I didn't want to crash and injure my body any more after my knee operation, but when we broke up I lost interest in trails and the jumps called me back. I pushed the Raptor until the crank broke, had it fixed under warranty, and then sold it to buy a Yamaha YFZ450. That quad had one of the best power to weight ratios available but more importantly it was the perfect machine to improve my freestyle jumping.

There is no bigger thrill I have come across in life than freestyle. There is so much risk involved but that is what lures people in to try jumping. When I line up for a ramp there is a commitment point, and if anything unusual happens past that point, or I abort the jump, I am going come up short and it will hurt. Every single time I jumped, it might have been the last time I walked or talked or did anything, and for an adrenaline junkie that is the ultimate rush.

My friend Chris was also a freestyle rider and we were a good influence on each other to test our growing skills. If he jumped something big, I needed to go bigger. We constructed big dirt ramps that grew by the day and got to the point of being unsafe, so we started to make solid ramps out of pallets. Hard ramps provided a more predictable surface so we could increase our speed and angles to get bigger air. I did a lot of learning with Chris and I was very lucky not to add more major injuries to my list as we learned how to soar through the air on motorcycles.

I was still living at home but after Dad sold the drag car our relationship deteriorated. After a big argument with him, I quit the nursery and moved out of home into Uncle Phil's house. Riding around Dad's land was not an option, so it did not take me long to notice Phil's neighbour had a freestyle ramp. I walked next door and introduced myself to Colin, who owned the ramps. Perth's freestyle scene is a small community and I found out Colin was friends with Chris, which helped in getting an invite to come over and have a ride. The first time I rode into Colin's ramp I knew it was what I needed to take my freestyle to the next level. The purpose-built structure gave a vastly different feeling to the dirt and pallets I had jumped before, throwing me into the air and doing a lot of the work for me. The ramps I had built absorbed my speed, so I needed to hit them faster, but Colin's curved ramp gave me precise air every time.

Colin introduced me to his friends Tristan and Ryan, who had a full size Aussie Comp-spec ramp. Ryan was jumping quads at a far superior level to my own and he was able to do the more complicated tricks like can-cans and supermans. I wanted to be able to perform stunts like those and I struggled to start with, but I just loved the feeling of air time. The more jumps I did, the more confident I felt to take on more difficult stunts and I became more comfortable with letting go of the handlebars in mid-air, kicking my legs to the side of the quad and doing all sorts of other ridiculous things. I sometimes didn't realise how high into the air I was getting until I looked back at footage from a GoPro or what my friends filmed. Flying on a bike and hanging off the back is a feeling I can't describe, you have to do it yourself.

I patched things up with Dad and he said I could come back to the nursery, both to ride and to work. I'd taken a job doing roof plumbing, but the nursery was where I wanted to be. Dad's bribe was pretty good, as he said he was going to pay me well and he even gave me a big sea container to tow to the back of the nursery where I could store all my freestyle stuff. My relationship with Dad has been defined by highs and lows; I rarely saw anything in between.

I returned to the nursery and thankfully Dad hadn't taken out our dirt jumps with a front end loader yet. We transformed the sea container into a bar so we could hang out in the back of the nursery and run amuck on our bikes. The nursery had a lot of old building materials sitting around and we found enough tin and wood to construct a lean-to on the shipping container. We thought we were honest-to-God legends with our own freestyle compound. We even picked up some old couches from a roadside rubbish collection, but they only lasted one night before being set on fire so we could do jumps over the top. My friend Craig remarked that the whole compound looked like something from the third world and we nicknamed the area

Freestyle riding consumed me, and with the space to practice I could grow my skills.

Shanti Town.

As time went on Shanti Town grew. Chris and I bought the Aussie Comp ramp from Tristan and Ryan to set up along with our pallet jumps. Dad had to sell the sea container but after some scavenging around the nursery we had found enough materials to build another bar. This time it was a proper stand alone structure, with tinned front and sides and even a beer garden – our idea of paradise.

With my own practice area my freestyle riding began to improve and, miraculously, Dad was on board. He had been talking with his friend Monk who told him about a big rock concert and dirt drag racing event he was working on called Westdale Rock. They wanted a freestyle show as part of the day's entertainment and Monk thought I could put on my first professional display with my friends. Monk's a big guy – a bit of an outlaw – and he was one of the few people Dad listened to, so for the next four months I could use the back of the nursery to prepare our show. The boys and I trained relentlessly so we could learn some stunts that would impress a crowd.

We travelled to Westdale a week before the show to prepare our ramps. Chris began to practice and looked good until he lost his balance mid-air on one of his jumps and came crashing back to Earth. The hard clay struck him like concrete as he tumbled, breaking both of his wrists and planting his face into the ground. Chris did not look well and we took him to Beverley Hospital where, as he ate through a straw, he decided he was retiring from freestyle riding.

I had never seen an accident quite that bad in person and when I tried to go back to practice I couldn't do it. Performance anxiety racked my mind and I worried I would not be able to do any stunts at my first freestyle gig. A couple of my friends joined the show to replace Chris and their confidence fortunately helped get my head straight.

We reached show day and I wanted to start on a positive note, but instead I over-jumped and landed near the bottom of the down ramp, snapping the chassis – now I had a broken quad to go with shaky confidence! Maybe the universe was giving me warning signs about freestyle. I thought my day was over, but thankfully one of the Westdale Rock organisers had a welder on site and he was able to make some quick repairs.

My friend Magilla took the lead while I waited for my quad to be fixed and as I watched him reel off some pro-level tricks something clicked in my brain. The pumping music and the big crowd made enough adrenaline flow through me to commit to my first jump back and everything gelled. Soon I was hanging supermans, doing big can-cans, clicking my heels; I was far off the pros, but it looked cool to most people and the show was a solid, if not smooth, success.

After Westdale Rock I was actually a little tired of riding. We'd been flat out for months improving our skills and while I didn't give up, I realised I wasn't any sort of pro showman despite the many hours of practice. Even with Westdale done, Dad still seemed cool with us riding at the nursery and I thought we were finally getting back to a stable relationship.

I mentioned earlier how I first started to experience people using me just so they could ride at the compound. One of those people did a burnout in the middle of the nursery one day when they were leaving, a really disrespectful act. We all did burnouts from time to time of course but for someone to do one at the business was not on. I immediately told Dad I'd get the high pressure cleaner to wash off the rubber, while he and Uncle Kim went to 'get up' the guy who'd done the skid. But something triggered in Dad's head at that moment and I don't know what it was to this day. He lost his shit, climbed into a front end loader and demolished Shanti Town, running over the bar and the jumps. He smashed everything before pushing the rubble into a heap and leaving it there. We had a big argument and I questioned what else I could have done, not knowing this guy was going to do a burnout in the first place? Our relationships was at the extremes, from him encouraging me to pursue freestyle to destroying the compound where I practiced.

It wasn't the only time Dad was destructive when he was angry. When the nursery was established in Serpentine, the nearby pub became a regular hang out for friends, staff from the nursery and I every Friday afternoon. The pub was located in a quiet country town on the outskirts of Perth and we'd run rampant, doing big burnouts along the main road. There was rarely any attention from the authorities and two new rubber marks were laid down on the road every time someone left.

On one wild night we had a bright idea, letting my mate Ben surf the lid of an esky (that's a cooler for the Americans) in the tray of my Mazda Bravo ute while I did a burnout, with my buddy Fingers riding shotgun. We got to a roundabout where Ben bailed out of the back of the ute and I proceeded on, scorching the tyres to the steel belts, which left me with no traction. We came to an S-bend in the road and without any grip, the Bravo did a 360 degree spin into a muddy ditch. Ben abandoned the esky lid just in time, coming out safely, but the Bravo was now stuck. I looked at Fingers and asked if he was okay, and told him not to open the door. As soon as I said the bloke opens the door and water poured inside the cabin. Ironically, the Living End song *Who's Gonna Save Us* was playing at the time. I wanted to get the car out of the ditch as soon as possible just in case any cops came along. Fingers went to the back of the ute and got the esky out, which was full of alcohol. He threw the esky into a nearby paddock, with bottles going everywhere. I didn't know why, as cops were going to easily see all the booze close to the accident scene.

I ran to the nearest property I could find and knocked on the door. An old bloke named Joe answered, and I asked if he could help us out. He said no worries and used a snatch strap behind his van to gently tug the stranded Bravo out of the ditch. The car looked okay and when I turned the key the motor started up just fine. I said thank you to Joe and was on my way, though Joe said he would follow behind to make sure we got home safely. Fingers said that Joe was going to dob us into the cops, and I had better floor it. So I put the foot down, with sparks flying off the steel belts left from the tyres as we got away.

The only evidence of the night's craziness was some water inside the headlights. But that was all it took to provoke Dad into taking an axe to the Mazda, smashing the windscreen and body panels. Both he and I were furious at each other. I was a wild young man, a product of the environment he and the family raised me in, but Dad couldn't find ways to deal with my behaviour without crossing into violence.

Fight of My Life

Despite the ongoing anger I felt toward Dad, I kept going to work. I wanted the nursery to succeed and I still loved the people in there enough to keep showing up. After another day on the job I went home for a shower, where I was having a good old wash when I noticed something on my right testicle. It was a hard lump, just under the skin. I really didn't think too much more about it, figuring it would be one of those things that went away.

The lump grew noticeably in size with each day. "OK, maybe I'll take care of it soon," I thought. Three weeks passed and the nut became brutally painful. Every time my balls so much as swung past my thigh it was agonising. I waited until the weekend to call my girlfriend at the time, Jess, to ask what I should do. She was in Bali but urged me to see a doctor immediately. Being a typical 22-year-old male, I waited until Tuesday because what's another couple of days, right? On the first examination the doctor didn't like what he saw and he referred me straight to a radiology clinic. They performed an ultrasound, after which they told me I needed to see a urologist as soon as possible because something abnormal had showed up on the scans. It was not their job to say I had cancer, but I heard a seriousness in how they talked that told me this was not a simple lump. I didn't have that sinking feeling yet; I was just thinking about getting to the next appointment to see what they could tell me for sure.

The ultrasound people wanted me to get another referral, but instead I went to the emergency ward at Murdoch Hospital, where urologist Dr Shane La Bianca was on the staff. If there's something wrong with anything in the vicinity of your underpants, he's your man. By the time I introduced myself to Dr La Bianca I could hardly walk due to the pain. The ultrasound showed two tumours in the testicle: one had a smooth surface and was predicted to be benign, while the rougher texture of the second indicated it was possibly cancerous. Dr La Bianca explained that a biopsy would be necessary to know for sure, and because of the tumours' size the whole testicle was going to have to come out. He told me testicular cancer was one of the most curable cancers and, if I was lucky, I might not even need chemo. He wanted to perform the surgery literally the same day I met him, such was the seriousness of the tumour; I had little time to consider the ramifications. They didn't know if the tumour was cancerous until it was removed from the scrotum, so there was no talk of saving the testicle.

The pain meant I was happy for an immediate solution, even one so drastic and permanent. Losing a testicle seems like it should have been a dramatic event, but something alien was inside me and I wanted it gone. In situations where there is a tough, but obvious decision to make I don't give myself a chance to doublethink. Whether the tumour was cancerous or not, it was causing me pain and it had to come out. I didn't agonise over a situation with only one outcome because I saw no point.

I sometimes wonder if being able to disconnect from the

emotion of a decision so readily is a positive or a negative in my personality. I don't consider myself a selfish person, but to truly succeed you need to have some kind of selfishness. In my life, I've treated some people like that testicle, cutting them off and casting them aside, but they are not rash decisions – just clean cut and permanent ones.

In the blink of an eye, I was in surgery. The doctors made an incision in the bottom right hand area of my groin, snipped and tied the spermatic cord, and then removed the testicle. Happy days! I thought my pain would be over when I woke up but recuperating from the operation was just as bad. I never realised how much pressure gets applied to the groin in daily actions like laughing, coughing or sneezing. Among my family and friends the next 'one ball' joke was never far away so I had to control my reactions to their humour until I was healed.

I definitely knew my testicle was gone. At the time I felt kind of violated, but it's hard to even remember what it was like living with two balls now. The human body is good at adapting, one ball does the job, and there's much more to being a man than my bits being in the right order.

I checked in with Dr La Bianca after the operation, while the biopsy was taking place. After we talked about the surgery he opened the top drawer of his desk and picked up a silicone ball, which he bounced on the desk for effect. "Have you considered a prosthetic testicle? There are three different sizes," he explained. The opportunity for pranks sprang to mind as I imagined putting a fake ball into a vice at parties to get a laugh, and I could get the big ball to make me braver, right? In the end I said I wasn't interested, pranks aside.

I awaited the biopsy results with a mixture of nerves and hope. Perhaps my enjoyment of freestyle jumping had taught me to keep my thoughts positive, no matter what the odds were. The results came back, and there it was: cancer. The tumour had grown incredibly fast in just three weeks and the aggressive nature of the cancer raised concerns on how far it had already travelled through the rest of my body. I don't care how tough you are, hearing a doctor say you have cancer shuts you up. "OK, I have cancer, now what?" I thought to myself. This was a fact I couldn't change and while I could cry or scream or tell Dr La Bianca to scan again, none of that was going to help. What would be, would be.

Cancer is a disease that tends to hit older people. Less than four percent of cancer occurs in people under 34. But my number was up, so what could I do? I'd rather know everything about a problem and set goals to create a resolution. I couldn't fix a problem with worry, only by moving forward with the right decisions.

I wasn't shocked I had cancer, but its rapid spread was a surprise. I'd prepared myself for the worst mentally so I could come into the situation looking up. If I hoped I didn't have cancer before receiving the results the bad news would have felt worse.

My next appointment was with an oncologist, Dr Sanjay Mukhedkar. His office was across from Dr La Bianca's, so it was literally out one door and in another. I have massive respect for Dr Mukhedkar to this day. He was very understanding, but at the same time he didn't give me any bullshit. He explained everything in depth so I knew all the information, while not hitting me with too many blows to my confidence. Oncologists become skilled at delivering bad news.

Right from the first appointment, he laid out a plan so we could beat the cancer. "You've got a big mission ahead of you," Dr Mukhedkar said. "So heads down, bums up, let's get this happening." I might be paraphrasing – but you get the gist.

I didn't know how serious this was all going to be, cancer was new to me. But when Sanjay laid down the line it put me in the mindset of going to war. I've never been to war, but it was what I imagined, being given a few tools and some odds of success. Here's my gun, here's my backpack, here's my mission, off I go.

I first needed more scans to establish how far the cancer had spread. Blood tests came first, followed by a CT scan, where my body was passed through a machine that looked like a giant medical donut. A total body PET scan was next, which required an injection of fluorodeoxyglucose – a radioactive sugar. Cancer loves feeding off sugar, so where ever cancer was in my body, the radioactivity of the fluorodeoxyglucose would light up green in the scan. After the injection, I had to sit still for an hour before I was laid down on a conveyor belt and moved into the PET scanner. This machine was far more intimidating than the CT scan, with my whole body in a tube maybe a metre wide. I wouldn't consider myself claustrophobic, but as I rolled inside the scanner with my nose almost touching the top of the tube I felt my muscles tense. I noticed that the other end was open, so I tilted my head back and focused on looking towards the opening. I relaxed and waited for the machine to do its work, scanning my body from head to toe.

After the scan I could finally move again, but I felt sick from the sugar running through my body. They offered me a cup of tea and some foul smelling sandwiches. People talk about hospital food but these were the worst sandwiches I ever had, some kind of pickled gherkin relish and 'meat'. I scraped everything off and only ate the bread, wondering what kind of hate-filled person could make this stuff.

Dr Mukhedkar called me into his office when he received the results of the scan. Green areas (showing cancer) glowed on the screen from where my testicle had been all the way to the bottom of my torso. Cancer has four stages doctors use to describe the severity of the condition. T1 is very superficial and not yet attacking deeper tissue, while T4 is terminal. I was at T3 testicular cancer, meaning I was still curable, but the cancer had spread beyond the initial tumour and was now invading other areas of my body. As I absorbed the information, Dr Mudhedkar started explaining the cure. I was to be given four doses of heavy chemotherapy, then my body would be scanned again to see if the cancer had been successfully eliminated or if I required further treatment. He was confident and competent, which were invaluable to me for my battle ahead.

My grandfather was a hardworking man killed by cancer. He had testicular cancer first, which he survived, but later in life stomach cancer got him. He worked like a mule, even after doctors had put a stent into his body to make his bile go around his stomach. One day he was pushing a heavy bale of hay off the back of a ute and the stint was dislodged, after which he went into hospital and never came back home. I didn't know how cancer was spreading through my own body, but I figured some rest and a calm mind couldn't hurt, so I avoided exercise or other exertion as I waited for treatment to begin.

After dealing with the initial shock of how advanced the cancer was, the positive side of my personality kicked in. I'd heard about how devastating chemotherapy could be, the way it shuts down the body and progressively made the patient sicker, to where their body felt like it was dying – because it basically was. An arrogant part of me started looking forward to the personal challenge. I wasn't a withered old man in the fading light of his life, I was young and I had a worker's body. I thought I was tougher than all the other people I'd known with cancer. This was like a boxing match and I was convinced cancer wasn't going to put me on the canvas.

Aussie band the Divinyls sung: "It's a fine line between pleasure and pain." I guess I could say the same about testicular cancer as my next stop was at Hollywood Private Hospital where I was to provide a sperm sample. There were two reasons for this. Firstly, it gave a sperm count to make sure everything was functioning as normal in my remaining testicle, and secondly, my sperm was frozen for use in the future if something abnormal happened, like the cancer spreading and rendering me impotent.

I went to the hospital with Jess for the unique experience. I'd never donated sperm, so this was all new to me. As we walked into the clinic we were making the immature jokes you'd expect, wondering if the nurse would ask, "Do you need a hand?"

I was a man on a mission. If donating sperm was going to be the first step to beating cancer then so be it. The nurse at the clinic gave me a plastic specimen jar, and politely explained that the semen had to be completely in the cup. I hated to think of the problems this bloke had dealt with in his career.

"Now, we have four drawers of selections for you," he said. Oh, here we go. "The first drawer is just female magazines, doing things to themselves and so on." Sounds good. "The second drawer is male and female." I could work with that. "The third drawer is male and male." Jess and I sniggered like school kids. "The fourth drawer has DVDs." For when you really mean business, I suppose.

I decided I could handle this myself (so to speak), so I left Jess at reception while I took care of business, in what was an unexpected start to my battle with cancer. Every Wednesday for three weeks I had to go in for the same appointment so they could monitor the sperm count accurately. I could only hope the rest of my mission would be so easy.

The countdown to chemo begun. I didn't fear the treatment, I just wanted to get it done and out of the way so I could move on with my life. I understand how people think the worst when they receive a cancer diagnosis, but when I was given facts that were outside of my control I believed I needed to fight against those emotions. Perhaps I'm lucky, because I feel like I saw chemo as a path ahead. Cancer wasn't on my long term agenda.

When Grandad was getting chemotherapy for his cancer, I remember Dad saying: "As soon as you have that big red bowl over your head you will never be the same again." I was seven or eight years old at the time, and I may not have heard or interpreted the words right, so for some reason I imagined the red bowl very literally. The machine survived in my memory and I went to my own chemotherapy expecting to be laying on a bed with a clear glass bowl over my head, watching red liquid drain into my veins. I had the bed part right, but chemotherapy looked just like an IV. A drip stand was plumbed into my arm, from which the nurses hung different bags of chemicals, customised for my treatment. It was time for the mission to truly begin.

The first bag was steroids, not the cheating-at-sports kind but corticosteroids that control allergic reactions, decrease nausea from other chemicals and deter white blood cells from heading towards the cancer by reducing swelling. As the drip begun I immediately felt nauseous, and with 'steroids' being the only chemical name I recognised I worried about what the other bags would feel like. As the bag emptied into my veins I felt sleepy and once the steroids finished I actually felt better. I thought back to how Dad had described chemo and I realised it was all fluff, pretending to know what he was talking about.

After the steroids came the serious stuff: etoposide, cisplatin and shots of bleomycin. Chemotherapy works by killing cells as they divide in the body. Once we are adults, most of our cells don't need to divide or multiply, with exceptions such as blood cells or hair follicles. Cancer is made up of cells that have begun to divide uncontrollably, causing tumours. If the cells can be killed as they divide, the cancer can be defeated, though that causes collateral damage to cells like the hair follicles, which is why people undergoing chemo lose their hair.

I found it empowering to understand how the chemotherapy chemicals worked. Bleomycin for example was extracted from a soil fungus, and once in my bloodstream it would bind itself to the DNA of my cells and break up the strands. It then inhibited the synthesis of DNA which resulted in the death of the dividing cell. A normal cell in the human body can repair itself from this damage, but if the cell was dividing (cancerous or otherwise), the bleomycine would kill it.

The steroids were pumped into me rapidly, but the bags of chemo were slow. I listened to the machine clicking as it pushed the chemical through a few drips at a time. I counted the clicks and wondered how long 1000 would take, or how many clicks would empty the bag. I had to stop myself from click counting before I went insane and looked elsewhere to pass the time. Daytime TV was always an option, where I became an expert on Ready, Steady, Cook and The Bold and The Beautiful. Anything I could focus on besides the progress of the chemo was a blessing.

The more potent chemicals didn't have immediate side effects, so I just had to be patient as the bags emptied. Once each bag was finished, the machine activated an alarm and I had to wait for the nurse to arrive. If I had a room to myself, I sometimes waited an hour for her to come back, all the while being tortured by the incessant beeping. I preferred the chemo lounge, where I was among other patients but didn't have to wait nearly as long. It was a strange atmosphere there, a whole bunch of people in comfortable chairs receiving toxic chemicals. The final bag given to me was potassium, which functioned as a cleanser to clear out my veins, and with that I had completed my first dose of chemotherapy. "That wasn't so bad," I thought to myself, pleased with my early performance in this fight. We left the hospital and Jess took me to Subway, though with the lingering effects of the nausea caused by the steroids I ate a little less than normal.

I was given a choice of staying in the hospital between my chemo doses or going home after the treatment. I figured hospital would be a relatively stress free environment to rest for a few days and I made plans to return home for the weekends. In those first days after the chemo, I didn't notice many changes. I felt tired, enough to know that I was on something, but my hair hadn't fallen out and I wasn't losing weight. I rested as much as I could and my only activity was going out for drives with Jess, sometimes visiting friends or getting a meal. I'd won this first round but I had some uncertainty in my mind. How would the future doses affect my body and, ultimately, would the chemo work or was this all going to be for nought?

Doubters and Dysfunction

The news of my cancer magnified the personalities of my family. Uncle Kim and Uncle Phil both responded well. They knew I had a plan for how I wanted to go through the treatment and their support gave me confidence. I always relied on my uncles to bring me back in line if I strayed. Lots of other family and friends sent me messages telling me to stay positive, convinced I was going to get through my chemo and beat cancer.

My relationship with Mum became more complicated. Mum had a lot of drama in her life, and I believe part of her personality indulged in it. She has a lot of love for all of her kids, but she had a way of orbiting the issues of my life without ever reaching a solution that could help. Mum and I dealt with problems very differently.

When there is a problem in our lives, we have the option to draw circles or lines. Lines take us from one place to another, perhaps to a solution or maybe to a different problem. Circles feel like they take us somewhere to begin with, but then they just bring us back to the same place we started; at best they are introspective. I drew lines and Mum drew circles, we just had very different characters and still do.

Mum and Dad's relationship has been very hot and cold

since I can remember. She was often kicked out of the house and I have childhood memories of staying at the Bentley Motor Inn near Perth Airport more than a few times. Dad supported Mum and she never had to work, so she kept the home tidy, cooked dinner and looked after us kids. But occasionally something would set Dad off and he would blow his temper, and sometimes they became physical in their arguments. I was only young, and so were my brother and sister, so what could we do? That was our normal. I've become aware of the effect the conflict had on me as I've grown older, and I now stop and consider the way I react to situations. Sometimes my temper will burn and I hear the echoes of my childhood, which makes me take pause to reflect on the traits of my parents' personalities that also exist in mine.

Despite the arguments and the fights, I felt like we were a strong knit family in the early days. We were spoiled with anything we asked for at Christmas. We had a holiday house in Exmouth we visited all the time and there were always fun gatherings between the different generations and arms of the family. Things changed when the nursery moved to Serpentine; I feel like that place was a cursed.

Mum was overwhelmed by the news of my cancer. In my mind I had a pathway ahead of me, I had the mission and I didn't want to look back. She was traumatised at the thought of losing a son to cancer, especially so young, and her emotions got the better of her, which made our relationship tense. Uncontrolled and negative emotion hindered my recovery and I wanted positive people to surround me during chemo. I hadn't counted on Mum's response and I felt an added burden from her emotion. To use the boxing analogy once more, I needed her at the sidelines cheering me on, but it felt like she was at the ropes in tears, asking for the fight to stop.

I can understand her perspective and my response may seem cold. Her son was in hospital getting treatment for a feared disease and she wanted to be there at every moment to show she cared, but I couldn't communicate to her what I needed. My advice for somebody trying to support a family member or friend with cancer is to really find out what they need from you, and give it to them. In my case, I had no need for overt displays of sad emotion to show love, what I needed were cheerleaders.

Dad and I were still barely talking after he demolished Shanti Town. Following the news of the cancer, he tried to make amends by giving me an open cheque to buy whatever materials I needed to rebuild, and he promised to pay for the cancer treatment. Like Mum, Dad had a hard time adapting to the news and providing the positive support I needed. I didn't want money, I needed him to back me up, yet I often felt like Dad had resigned himself to my decline and eventual death. It was negative energy I did not need; I had a fight on my hands.

I thought Dad would have been better prepared to help, given he was there for Grandad's chemotherapy, but our relationship became progressively worse. Maybe the fact that Grandad had passed away gave Dad little faith in my own strength or the effectiveness of the treatment.

He was under stress from many directions, one of which was needing to sell a block of land next door to the nursery. On the land was a motocross track I had carved from the dirt and he had asked me to level it out shortly before I had been diagnosed with cancer. As you can imagine, this job quickly became one of the last things on my mind.

Shortly after my first chemo treatment, Dad got into me about not demolishing the track. Operating heavy machinery wasn't on the list of activities the average chemo patient should be doing and we argued aggressively. The phone call ultimately finished with him telling me I needed to take all of my shit out of his house – I was getting kicked out of home in the middle of chemotherapy.

There was no way Dad was in his right mind, at least I hope not, because I don't see how he could treat a son like that. His confused actions while I was fighting cancer were the most damaging of all to our relationship, and it seemed he wanted to make my life as hard as possible. I needed to organise moving my things before he literally threw them on the kerb.

Together with Jess I took all my stuff from home and moved it into Jess's parents house and Nanna Val's house. Nanna wanted to help me out, because that's what Nannas do best. She also offered to look after my little dog Cooper. I didn't want to leave Cooper with Dad while he was angry, because there was no telling what he would do.

Jess was a life saver. She was a nurse and her experience dealing with patients made things so much easier for me. She stayed on top of the nurses treating me to make sure I was getting the best care, but she also gave me an insight into what the nurses went through themselves. Her positivity and optimism, along with her knowledge, helped push me through the journey. We had our differences, but without her help and being there for me, I think keeping my head up would have been extremely difficult. She was giving me every bit of positive thought I needed and even though Jess had never had cancer, she related to me – something I couldn't sense my parents doing. Perhaps it was just the fact she was a nurse, but her initial reaction was the same as mine: "Righto, let's get on with it." Her support was rock-steady which helped fill the gap left by Dad's behaviour.

In the days before my second dose of chemo my appetite began to fade and when I returned to the hospital I noticed odd symptoms for the first time. The chemo ward of the hospital had a small bakery next door and I loved the aromas when I walked past before my first treatment. This time the smell of the coffee and pastries hit me in the face and I wanted to vomit. I was dry retching, but I had nowhere to throw up so I held my breath just to make it past the bakery. I glanced sideways at a pastie and all I could think about was turnips and offal and whatever else they put inside them. It was the first strange side effect of chemo to happen to me and really took me out of my comfort zone. I loved those foods and I couldn't understand my reaction.

I went through the second round of chemo, the same order of chemicals as the first, and stayed in hospital for a couple of days to rest. Unlike my first dose, I begun to feel the effects on my body as the chemicals did their work. My appetite evaporated almost completely and I struggled to keep food down, but strangely I developed a taste for sushi. I'd never liked sushi before yet for some reason it was one of the few foods that made me feel hungry when I thought about it. "Delectable little snacks," I'd think to myself as I munched down.

I tried to stay awake as much as possible but I needed a lot of sleep, and my motivation to do anything else during the day waned. My physical activity became limited and I settled for walking around the pond at the hospital, checking out the ducks and seeing what they had to say. I ate some sushi and that was my whole day. I learned life in the hospital was much more enjoyable if I could get along well with the nurses, who were understanding and compassionate people. I was grateful for the people who were caring for me and I appreciated how their priority was entirely to their patients. They tried to keep everything as stress free as possible for me.

The chemo was taking control and changing things in my

body. I begun to feel melancholy set in as my serotonin and dopamine levels were affected. These neurotransmitters were among the dividing cells the chemo went after. I always had some kind of positive spirit through the treatment, but I could sense my emotional responses weren't as strong as they should have been. That was why I needed a positive and caring environment around me, and people who could understand how my treatment worked. My body couldn't physically be happy by itself.

Mum asked to come to the hospital while I was undergoing my chemotherapy, so I gave her the time when I was receiving my steroids. I could fall asleep while the drip was taking place and eventually she would leave the room and go home. That might seem cold hearted but she didn't know how to help me and her presence sometimes brought me down. The nurses were helpful and stayed around my room if my parents came while I was asleep – they couldn't be fooled. Despite my argu-

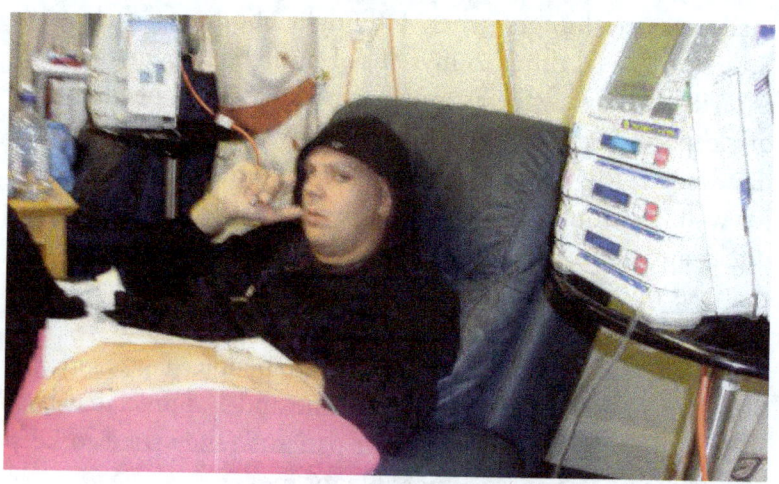

Chemotherapy, even less fun than it looks.

ments with Dad, he still visited. But his moods were unpredictable and I felt like I was either his beloved first born or the bane of his existence depending on the day.

After the second round of chemo, Jess and I drove back to her house from the hospital to spend a couple of days. I called Nanna to see how things were going with her and to check on how Cooper was; I was pretty keen to catch up with my little dog. "Cooper's gone missing," she told me. I wasn't greatly surprised, as Nanna lived on a 160 acre farm and Cooper had a lot of room to roam. He and Nanna's rottweiler went for walks together but they always returned home sooner or later. I told Nanna not to worry, and we drove to see her and Cooper, who I expected would be back by the time we arrived.

"Cooper's still not here," Nanna said when we pulled up, but I had a positive feeling he wouldn't be far from where his food was. I caught up with Nanna for a while but I soon felt exhausted from the effects of the chemo, and we drove back to Jess's parents house. I called Uncle Kim as we left and asked if he could drive around the farm to search for the dogs.

Forty minutes later Kim called back, with a seriousness in his voice. He found Cooper's body on a neighbouring property, where he'd eaten poison fox bait and died, together with Nanna's dog. As I heard Kim say the words I recognised what he said but I felt strangely emotionless. I knew I should have been upset, but my brain's chemicals had been eroded and unbalanced by the chemotherapy and I felt only emptiness. Kim asked what I wanted to do and I told him to meet me at Dad's house, which I still regarded as my family home even though I had been kicked out a few days earlier. We went to a garden bed a short distance from the house, where Kim dug a hole and laid my dog to rest, while Dad stood to the side. When I saw my little dog my heart broke; he still had blood on his nose from the effects of the bait. After I said goodbye to Cooper, I went back to Jess's house and I was beside myself as the sadness of the loss broke through the numbness of the chemo. That dog was my best mate and I can't explain enough how much I loved him.

Cooper didn't have to die. All I could think about was how Dad's demands for me to move out of home was what caused this. My emotions transformed from sadness to anger. I thought back to our argument over the phone, where I only needed a reasonable father. All I could think about was how all of this didn't have to happen. I had cancer, I was kicked out of home by my family and my dog had died – life just didn't feel fair.

I tried to keep my spirits up after Cooper's death. I went over to a mate's place and rode around on a quad briefly, even though I couldn't do much except for sit on the thing. Another friend had a birthday party in the city, so Jess and my sister Jodi organised a hotel room for us all. It was all fun until Jodi threw up in the hotel toilet enough to block it. When she passed out it was up to me to unblock a vomit-covered toilet bowl, while throwing up myself from the chemo.

I went back to hospital for my third chemo dose. I'd managed to get a few cheap shots in early against the drugs but the chemo was winding up for a knockout punch. I spent each day in hospital, returning to Jess's parents house at night.

Dad felt bad about what happened to Cooper and he called me after my third treatment to let me know he'd organised a surprise. He showed up at Jess's house with my Toyota Hilux, which he had organised to be beautifully modified with a hard top for the tray and some nice new wheels. The ute was painted purple with a blue metallic sparkle just like Dad's drag car and it looked amazing. I really liked it, but my reaction didn't show much emotion. I literally couldn't because the required chemicals weren't available in my brain – dopamine and serotonin release are impaired by chemotherapy. I was thankful and happy, but it was hard to be *physically* happy or sad about anything while I was on chemo and that was difficult to understand for healthy people. The process had physically and mentally drained me not just of my energy but of what my body needed to feel any emotion at all.

Dad expected different. He thought that I would forgive him upon receiving this gift, but my reaction was muted through the chemo. The situation became tense and he stormed off. I don't know how he expected someone in the middle of chemotherapy to react – jump in the air? Do a couple of backflips? Reach the stars, swing off the moon? I really did love what he had done to the car, but I couldn't show it and as he left my own emotions stayed numb, feeling neither the elation of his gift nor the insult of his departure. Not long afterwards I received abusive text messages where he called me an ungrateful cunt. Dad had a reputation among my family for using money and gifts to try and buy respect. I showed Jess the messages and felt like giving up on Dad entirely. "I don't need this shit in my life," I said.

The messages continued. Dad said he had to speak to me on the phone because he couldn't handle the smell of me on chemo. He told me I was 'chemo-fucked' and didn't know what I was talking about, and all because I didn't tap dance when he showed me the ute. Given the life events I was dealing with at the time, I don't think I could be held responsible for any negative reaction, much less an ambivalent one. Dad's focus seemed entirely on himself.

A week later he called me again. I didn't want to answer but Jess told me to get it over with. She was right, because he was just going to keep calling until I answered. He didn't ask me about the progress of my chemo or how I was feeling, but instead just asked how the ute was going. Then he told me to get all my stuff out of it because he was coming to pick it up later. I was confused and asked why he was coming to get my car, and the only reason he gave was that I already had a car – he was talking about Jess's car. With the way I was feeling, I couldn't have cared less about a car, even my own. I was prepared to do anything to have this negativity out of my life.

I told Jess to leave the keys in the car so I didn't have to see Dad; I couldn't be around him. He came and went, but a couple of hours later, Jess's father arrived home and came to talk with me.

"Ben, what is all this paperwork flying around the front yard? It's all your scripts and stuff," he said.

I looked at Jess in a moment of realisation and it dawned on me that I had left all my cancer paperwork in the car. People who are on chemo often have difficulty remembering things, trouble concentrating and processing information, and overall confusion. When Dad had picked the car up, he'd thrown all of my important papers out on to the driveway and driven off. Thankfully Jess's family rallied around me. They could not understand how this drama was happening, and how Dad seemingly forgot I was even undergoing treatment. Chemo was enough to deal with, let alone adding the stresses of a dysfunctional family.

It was time to dedicate my mind to turning off the negativity because the fight with chemo was becoming one sided. After the third dose my body was hammered and I started to go neutropenic as my white blood cell count dropped. I had no immune system left and I couldn't stop vomiting. Powerade was the only substance with any kind of energy that I could keep in my stomach for a short time, but even that eventually came up too. I was spewing so bad I couldn't breathe, bringing up bile between gasps. I was too exhausted to move from Jess's bed. Jess's father checked on me and decided enough was enough, he legitimately thought I was dying and rushed me to Murdoch Hospital, where the staff were shocked at my rapid deterioration. There I was put on to an IV drop immediately to start feeding and hydrating me and they explained how even a common cold at this stage might have been enough to kill me. The chemo had got the better of my body and I was admitted to hospital for recovery. Barely two months had passed since discovering the cancer and now I was as close to the edge of death as I had ever been, or have been since – and still with no guarantee I was cancer free.

Dr Mudhedkar came to see how I was doing and after seeing my condition he didn't want to put me through the planned fourth dose of chemotherapy. "The third one nearly got you," he said. Before I started chemo, Dr Mudhedkar had warned me that I would never experience anything as bad in my life. He was right, and it showed me the limits of the human body. It was like having the worst hangover of your life combined with the flu and it wasn't going away until I was finished with the chemicals.

My veins were so badly deteriorated from the chemo that they had collapsed and it was hard to even find a vein to insert my cannula for the IV. The nurse, who looked like she might have been an East German shot-putter in the seventies, was training and the staff figured I made a perfect candidate for her to learn on. She thought she finally found a vein and began the drip, but then a huge mass formed in my arm as liquid filled the space between my muscle and skin. It was painful as hell.

"Stop, stop!" I yelled, drawing the attention of the other nurses in the ward. I might have been lacking emotion and energy but the anger boiled easily. I shook my head and said I did not want that nurse near my IV for the rest of my stay.

I recovered gradually as the chemicals from the chemotherapy left my body. Dr Mudhedkar wanted a final PET scan before I left to determine if the chemo had worked, and he sent me home to await the results.

Soon I had the news: the chemo dose I was given had been sufficient to kill the cancerous cells in three months! I was at home when I received the results, but immediately put together a party to celebrate in style. I went to the fancy riverside restaurant Coco's for lunch and downed a bottle of Moet champagne afterwards in the shower. I had remained confident and upbeat

After my cancer-free diagnosis, Phil Preedy from Toyotaways Rockingham asked what my favourite AFL team was. I was surprised to meet Fremantle Dockers player Aaron Sandilands.

through the whole treatment, but to get the results back was still the single greatest relief I have ever felt. "I beat cancer. I'm young and invincible!" I thought to myself.

To celebrate my cancer free diagnosis, I bought a new quad from Canada and I took it to Uncle Phil's Grand Final party, where I did a big wheelstand down his street, feeling completely unstoppable. I was keen to show off my returning strength and tried to do a handstand while doing the wheelie, only to lose control and fall on to the bitumen. I smashed my ankle badly and wore some road rash, with the quad finishing beyond repair. Yep, I was back to normal.

Fuel for Thought - II

After my chemotherapy I entered a five year remission stage, which I'm happy to say has remained cancer free. I never thought about the cancer coming back during that time. As I've grown older, I look at cancer differently. I believe everyone has the potential for cancer in their body, and I don't think I will live the rest of my life without cancer striking again. It could be tomorrow or it could be when I'm 80, presuming I make it that far.

That doesn't mean I see my life as futile, instead I use that prediction as fuel. When I was younger I did many of the things I wanted to do and thought I would be content with my life, even if the cancer did return. That's the beauty of being young, I thought I had everything worked out. I've grown older and now I look at my current girlfriend Tara and her kids, and I wonder about the impact on them if I had cancer again. Have I achieved everything I want to in this life? To me life is a race, where I have to accomplish as much as possible in the years I have been given. Some of us have a shorter race, and we don't get to find out when the race ends. So just run like hell I say.

From the time I received the diagnosis, to being told the cancer was in remission, my headspace was entirely around beating the disease. I couldn't control the sickness, but I could give myself the positive mindset to make a difference, and there's fewer challenges tougher than cancer to test your willpower. I believe today that cancer taught me how to handle life's bigger issues, that you can move on with anything and get the job done. The experience I acquired then would continue to benefit me in the years to come.

Moving On

Beating cancer left me as wild as ever, and I sought to live every day to the maximum with a new found zest for the extremes of life.

The nursery was still operating, but things felt different. After my cancer was defeated, I had started up my own landscaping business, called Ace of Spades. I was picking up a decent amount of work thanks to my friend Plugger, who got me into the business and gave me lots of jobs.

Things remained inconsistent between Dad and myself and our relationship did not improve. Mum was struggling with her condition and the painkillers she took to control it. She was affected mentally and physically and that flowed on to Dad's behaviour. The costs of the nursery, including the hefty repayments for the German greenhouse, now outweighed the cash flow. The business had doubled in size but Dad and Uncle Kim had bitten off more than they could chew and the stress was showing. When Dad arrived at the nursery in the mornings he was more and more not himself, and Kim would shake a packet of Tic-Tacs when Dad came into the propagation area, insinuating Dad was on a combination of medication again.

The personal drama affected the people who were the fabric

of the nursery. Dad had a big fight with Mum and kicked her out of the house, then he went to Nanna Jean and Mike's house and kicked his in-laws out too. They were in their seventies and had sold up everything they owned to come and live at the nursery and help the family business. That was the final straw for Mike, who said he was never coming back to the nursery.

The incidents became dangerous. Dad got into an argument with my sister Jodi and pointed an air rifle at her. She called the police and the next thing you know the road outside the house was closed down and the Police Tactical Response Group had been called in.

The financial and personal pressure around the nursery came to a head. The family had a holiday house in Exmouth which was taken by the bank, as money had been borrowed against it for the nursery. Things around the business started to be forgotten and, worst of all, people weren't being paid. My cousin Brod, who was meant to inherit the family business like me, could see the writing on the wall. He wasn't being paid and had to quit, because he had a mortgage to pay.

I landscaped by myself a couple of days a week, then worked at the nursery for the rest of the week, but my pay was becoming unreliable like everyone else's.

Dad was getting desperate because staff were leaving, and he asked me if I could get some people to help. He promised to pay and I wanted to be there to help Uncle Kim, so I agreed. I organised a small crew of friends and acquaintances and we started moving some plants around the nursery.

Not long into the new crew's employment, Dad came roaring down the main driveway of the nursery in a big tip truck, while I was riding a quad in the opposite direction with three trailers attached, carrying my crew and plants. As we got closer I could see he was going too fast and we were going to hit, so I swerved right off the road as the truck came within inches of running over the rear trailer one of my workers was sitting in. I came to a stop in a bed of plants with everyone shocked about the near miss; I'd hate to think what could have happened if the truck had rolled over the trailer with my worker aboard.

I was livid. I'd gone out on a limb with these new people to help Dad out, I wasn't getting paid, and now he wanted to carry on with this reckless behaviour. I angrily trod to where Dad got out of the truck. "What the fuck are you on? You just about killed my worker," I yelled. "Start thinking about what you are doing."

Dad told me to fuck off out of the nursery. I loaded everything back on the trailers and carried on, wanting to get my job finished so Kim wasn't left with the workload. I returned back to the work area near a bed of plants where all of the staff were and began loading the trailers. Dad came to the shed and yelled at me to get off his property. "I'm here to help Kim, not you," I said.

Dad moved to slap me with his hand. My boxing experience kicked in when he let fly, and I punched him in the jaw, knocking him out. It was the first time we'd had a physical confrontation as adults and silence fell among the workers in the shed. All of the Bali workers were still there, loyal to the nursery's end, but Dad had been treating them like shit and they weren't getting paid reliably either.

"Young Boss got one up on Botak," Bucktooth Buzzard said quietly. Botak means bald in Indonesian.

Dad had an ambulance take him away, and when he returned he called the police and had a violence restraining order taken out on me. I gathered all of my things and moved out of home again, figuring I had finally reached the end of my life at the nursery.

I started working with my brother-in-law at a demolition company to get ahead, still out of pocket from the nursery. I was surprised when Dad got in touch. He seemed to have a clear head and said he was feeling bad about things and wanted to make amends. He said I could take plants to the markets to recoup the money I was owed, and as long as I gave him and Kim a little bit on the side for their costs, we could call it even. I thought I would never go back to the nursery but the offer was too good to refuse and I started working seven days a week, demolishing Monday to Friday and then spending my weekends at the markets selling plants. It was another perfect example of the ups and downs in Dad's personality, where an act that seemed so strange or erratic was followed by another of sense and reason. I remained wary.

On a good day at the markets I could make a week's wage. Little old Asian ladies opened up purses full of cash and I sold them conifers, exotics and shrubs. I had to teach myself how to sell and I learned a lot at the markets, interacting with customers and experiencing the respect they needed. I was also discovering what varieties were selling and what weren't, because like any other product plants followed trends. Even though I wasn't working at the nursery at the time, I still wanted to see it succeed for the family. I passed on the sales information but it was all too little too late.

The business had spiralled out of control, to where no recovery was possible. More family assets were sold to try and keep bankruptcy at bay. My ute was repossessed because it was under the business, even though I made the repayments to the nursery; but the repayments weren't going from the business to the car loan. All the houses, land and equipment was sold off. Much of the nursery business was in my Nanna's name and she was eventually declared bankrupt and her house was taken by the bank, in a time of great stress for the family. She lived with Uncle Kim for 10 months before she was put into a retirement home. Some months later, Kim found her dead on the floor from a heart attack. Like my Grandad, her life had been the nursery, and it was sad she had to see it collapse before her peace.

The nursery was interwoven with all of our lives, it was who the family was in many respects. It represented our success and now our failure, made all the harder as it ultimately fell from within. I had to look at my life from a different perspective and I transformed the problem to possibilities. If the nursery was still running, there's a high chance I would still be there today, even with Dad and I's rocky relationship. Instead I would have to go my own way and discover what I was capable of myself.

First Strike

Shortly before the nursery had closed for good, I begun getting back into freestyle, and I wanted to find a more stable place to cut loose on my quad and improve my skills. Uncle Phil had land in Forrestdale and after some sweet talking from me he was good enough to let me run amuck and build a new freestyle compound there.

We moved a sea container on to the land and built a tin roof lean-to for a bar area, proclaiming a second Shanti Town. This patch of backyard engineering was heaven to us. We created a massive down ramp for us to land on, with several launching ramps placed next to one another to hit; we even poured a small concrete burnout pad to thrash on. This was the Shanti Town I had dreamed of and every Friday afternoon we'd have some drinks and practice freestyle. We were out of everyone's way with only our own safety to be concerned about (or not).

There was nowhere else in Perth to do this. We couldn't legally build a jump or take a ramp into the public off road tracks. Word spread around the freestyle and motocross community and I had many people asking to come to Shanti Town to ride

I paid for it all from my own pocket with the help of a few favours from friends, but my plans were ahead of my wallet.

I decided to have a little show out there later in the year and charge people admission with the idea to funnel all the funds back into Shanti Town – like some kind of hoon's paradise, or extreme sport not-for-profit.

Planning for the first party began. One of my good mates, I can't mention his name, had a contract removing liquor that was past its use-by date from licensed venues. Hating to see such a resource wasted, I offered the expired grog a good home and filled a 40 feet-long sea container with expired cartons of Budweiser, Emu Export and Tooheys Extra Dry.

I advertised a freestyle motocross show, with a couple of burnout cars and all-you-can-drink alcohol. I planned for just friends and family to attend but I soon had a list 200 people long, all expecting a gnarly time – and I gave them one. It was like a buck's party on steroids with booze, dirty girls and all the rest. The day ran professionally with a guest list at the front gate, even a water truck to keep dust down and make sure the neighbours weren't disturbed. No one was hurt or injured (always a plus with freestyle) and it was just a good day all round. I threw great parties but made a terrible accountant – when I did the sums, I'd made exactly $10.

The new Shanti Town allowed me to get better at freestyle and three years after my first show at Westdale, I was lucky enough to land a booking at the Motorcycle and Scooter Show at Perth Convention Centre. The organisers were reaching out for freestylers to put on some demonstrations and got in touch with my friends Brett and Lorraine at Legend Quad Services, who suggested my show. I had a new quad, an absolute animal with all the latest gear, and as one of the few quad freestylers in WA I considered myself a bit of a legend. I gave the organisers a list of stunts I could do and they were keen to have me involved.

I went to the Convention Centre to check the location before the show. I borrowed Colin's up ramp and a portable down ramp had been set up by the two-wheel freestyle guys. The show organisers said I could use my own ramp, but I figured theirs would work well enough, even though it wasn't designed for a quad. A practice session was scheduled for Thursday before the event opened to the public, but it began to rain and we had to stop part way through. I had just a brief chance to check out the ramps before the wet weather and worked on my speeds and angles. It wasn't the perfect set up for me but I could get by.

The following day, I was on my way back to the Motorcycle and Scooter Show when I saw my Uncle Eddy driving a front end loader slowly along the road. I hung out the side of my car and gave him the finger, being a silly bugger. We were always smartasses to each other. He laughed when he saw me and I told him I was off to do some freestyle stunts.

"Don't go breaking your fucking legs!" he joked.

"Shut up old man, you don't know anything!" I yelled back.

I arrived at the Convention Centre where the doors were opening for the first official day of the show. A steady stream of people arrived to look at all kinds of two wheeled vehicles and enjoy the entertainment. I ran some spanners over my quad and gave it a cursory check over, but there would be no time for practice – it was show time. I stood back as the rest of the freestyle boys did their warm up jumps before I fired up my quad and accelerated for my run into the jump. Motor revving and ramp approaching, I committed to the jump at the same time I realised I was going too fast. I had little experience jumping on concrete and the hard surface allowed me to build up speed quicker than normal. I flew through the air and sailed over the safety of the down ramp, flat landing the quad on the concrete.

As every kind of shock absorption in the suspension bottomed out, I felt my left leg snap and right ankle blow out. A mental picture of the x-rays went through my head as I came to a stop. I rode as best I could back to the pit area and the concerned looks of the other riders. "You guys better get me an ambulance quick smart," I said.

I rested on the seat of my quad and almost fell straight off the back; the whole subframe was broken. My brother-in-law Aaron and mate Fingers were there and they said they had missed seeing the stunt, but they heard the engine revving in the sky, followed by a crack, and they knew it was bad. The paramedics arrived to administer painkillers and send me to Royal Perth Hospital (is anyone still keeping count of hospital visits?), which was fortunately only a few blocks down the road.

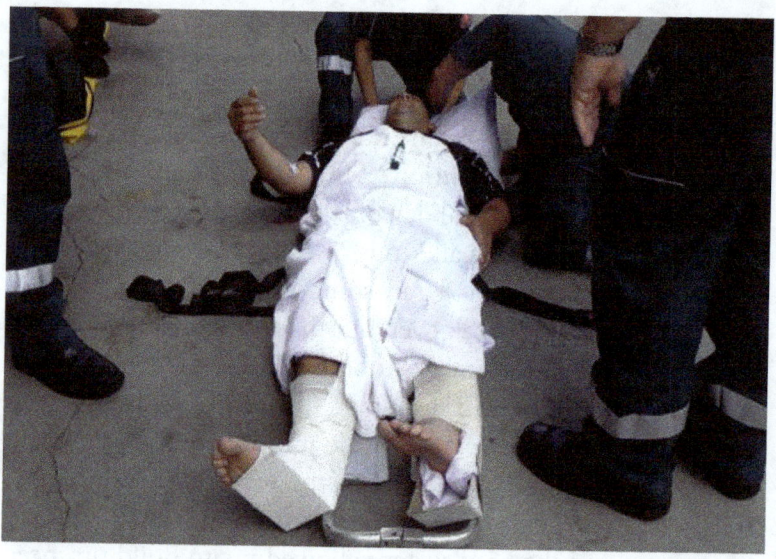

Getting attended to shortly after my first big crash, note the green whistle on my chest to ease the pain.

Doctors informed me I had a snapped tibia and fibula on my left hand side, while on the right side I had put the calcaneus (ankle bone) through the Achilles tendon, which made a real mess of the foot. Surgery was needed to add plates and screws to the ankle in an effort to get the bone to fuse, while my left leg received a rod from the knee to my ankle.

I steeled myself for a long stint in hospital with the memories of chemo still fresh in my mind, but I discovered the experience would be very different. I was relatively able bodied when I had cancer and the mental battle was to push through the treatment, which attacked the very way my brain operated. I could walk around outside if I wanted to feel the sunshine on my face, but sometimes the end seemed so far away.

This time my broken bones meant I couldn't run around all over the place to pass the days. But my mind was healthy and operational and now I had a waiting game as the bones healed. Boredom was the enemy, and I realised I had to work against negative thoughts which could have lead to depression. I never allowed my mind to feel like I was stuck in that bed and I told myself I was on a resort holiday where I listened to music and someone brought me food all the time. It wasn't exactly like going away to Bali but the mind trick helped.

When I had cancer, the hospital environment around me was very loving and caring. The cancer ward nurses spent a lot of time with people who had few days left to live; softly spoken and gentle, they knew the timeline for cancer meant even leaving the hospital was no guarantee of a full recovery. But as an injured stuntman the medical staff treated me differently. They'd call me a 'Temporary Australian', make jokes at my expense (and I returned the favour), and generally pushed me towards a point in time where my recovery would likely be complete.

I found ways to relieve the boredom. I made friends with all the nurses, which not only made the day go faster, but also made them more keen to make me toast and cups of Milo. I found a little bit of respect and common courtesy got me a long way in the public health system. I watched other patients get in there and have a whinge, feeling like they were owed something, but it never helped them. My positive mindset also did much to help my own physical healing. I had a couple of weeks to pass in Royal Perth Hospital before I was handed over to the Shenton Park rehabilitation facility to start some physical therapy. I had the same boredom there, though learning how to use a wheelchair entertained me – at least it was on wheels.

The fellow patients I met in Shenton Park were interesting to me, everybody had their own story and their own way of dealing with their problems. Some took it on the chin as one of life's troubles while others struggled to adapt to their new normal. One young fella in the bed next to me was very depressed about his future. He had been in a high-speed road bike accident, after stealing a motorcycle from the front of a bottle shop while under the influence of meth. He told anyone who would listen about his sad story, about how unlucky he was, and questioning why this event had befallen him. He even believed someone had knocked him off the motorcycle, and that it wasn't his fault, though that didn't appear to be the case.

We had a doctor in common, Professor Rene Zellweger. He was very helpful to my recovery and he took no prisoners; he didn't mince words with his patients. One day Zellweger tired of this kid's stories and tore strips off him, telling him how the hospital had the toxicology reports and they knew exactly what happened. He really set this kid straight, and said whining to all the nurses about the circumstances wasn't going to do a damn thing to help his recovery. The words hit me too, and it really dawned on me for the first time how my choices meant I owned not just the reward, but the consequences.

The highlight of Shenton Park was my new mate Clem. He was an old bloke with a broken femur who thought the world revolved around him, and he'd been in rehab for a while. He thought his long stay gave him more rights than anyone else in the hospital and I had the joy of sharing a room with him, along with two other patients. All Clem wanted was more morphine and he groaned and writhed constantly, acting like he was in pain. The nurses were well and truly on to his game though and they could tell from his biological signals that he wasn't in pain. Clem was just a nuisance.

I was granted a few hours of leave during my stay and my girlfriend took me to the shops to get some fresh air. Who should we pass in the street but my mate Clem? He was getting pushed around in his wheelchair by some old dear and was double-fisting two long neck stubbies of beer in brown paper bags. Clem was having a good old time and was blind drunk. I had a laugh and went back to Shenton Park. Later I was in my bed resting and Clem returned, now on crutches instead of a wheelchair and swaying around the room, reeking of booze. God knows where he found those crutches; I think he might have stolen them from someone. I gave him a verbal prod from my bed. "Where's your wheelchair, Clem?"

"I don't need that wheelchair anymore!" he declared with bravado, throwing the crutches away. Clem disappeared from my sight as he fell to the ground, right at the foot of my bed. The nurses heard the crash and rushed in, asking Clem where he found crutches and why he smelt of beer. He was cut off from all painkillers afterwards and it was no coincidence he checked himself out from the hospital the next day.

Things were quieter with Clem gone. I wasn't able to do much physiotherapy yet because I was still so freshly broken and the nurses suggested I could be discharged to continue my recovery at home and come into the hospital for rehabilitation as required. I wasn't strong enough to go back to work and at home the boredom seemed worse, so I bought a Toyota Hilux ute to work on. It was a little ripper of a car and my friend Scott talked me into putting a bigger motor into it, which helped pass the time as my leg healed. We put a four-litre Lexus V8 under the bonnet and made a sweet burnout machine.

Three months after I finished the motor conversion on the Hilux my legs had healed enough to go back to working with my brother-in-law Aaron. I tried to keep moving during my recovery, because I thought more blood flowing past the injury would help it heal. There are probably many human biology experts who would disagree with my theory but it seemed to work for me. I stayed active and found out how much my body could take, testing my strength more each day. When I returned to work at the demolition company I was straight on a jackhammer and pushing wheelbarrows. My leg had been broken and snapped many times but it was exceedingly strong, because the mass of bone that had fused around the multiple breaks was huge.

Aaron invited me to the pub, where I got drunk and did a massive burnout in the Hilux when I left (the owner of the pub remembers it to this day, and now sponsors my drag bike). I was in no way fit to drive home, with a few drinks under my belt and sore legs, and I fell asleep behind the wheel on a major road, crashing into a street light.

Looking back now, I was doing a lot of stupid things trying to relieve the pressure of my accident recovery and the collapse of the family business. I was very lucky not to hurt myself or anyone else on the road that night.

Awoken by the crash, I groggily climbed out of the car to survey the damage. I'd only just started walking again and now here I was standing beside the road after a major wreck, which could have easily broken my legs again. Some passersby stopped to help, but I told them I would sort it out. Instead I walked up a nearby hill and hid out for a while in the night to consider my options. My sluggish, alcohol-affected brain realised that eventually a police car would pass and see the accident scene, or someone would report it, so I flagged down a driver who was kind enough to give me a lift to my girlfriend's house. The car was in her name so after I told her what happened we decided to go back to the wreck. We hauled the car out of the sand and just about had it ready to tow when a police car showed up, red and blue lights flashing. Needless to say, they had some pertinent questions and I had stupid answers.

"My girlfriend's car was stolen from The Gate," I said. "We were just driving home and saw it."

It wasn't my proudest moment and the cops gave me a disbelieving look. They took me to the police station where I blew over the legal blood alcohol limit.

I wasn't massively over the limit by the time of the test, so I decided to take it to court to see if I could argue my way out of it, not knowing when to give up. I had inherited Dad's disrespect for authority and I mucked the court around for as long as possible, getting the case adjourned and hoping it would all get too hard for them. My tricks were amateur at best and when I finally went to trial the judge threw the book at me. My driver's licence was suspended for two and a half years and I received a $7000 fine. My biggest mistake was telling a lie to the police, so let this be a lesson to you: it's a terrible idea to try and play the fool with the system.

I'd had all this time off work from the broken leg and now I wouldn't be able to get to work at all. I thought Aaron was going to kill me. Continuing to tempt fate, I borrowed my sister's car and I drove to work despite losing my licence. Fortunately I got a break from my bad luck – though I'm not sure I can reduce self-inflicted events to fortune. I was landscaping at a house and my mate Tim was giving me a hand for the day. We needed to go to Bunnings to get some supplies and I was going to drive without a licence again.

"For fuck's sake, Benny, you've got someone who can drive for you," Tim said, taking the keys. We didn't get two streets away before blue and red lights flashed behind us, with Tim driving and me in the passenger seat. It was the only time I have ever been happy to be pulled over.

Too Much Fun

Through my accident and recovery, the Shanti Town freestyle compound remained an enjoyable sideshow to my life. Our first party showed we could deliver some loose fun and word spread of the wild time everyone had. I was still in a wheelchair when we put on our second show, which was a success, as was a third show on Australia Day. We even raised $3500 for the Leukaemia Foundation. We felt very free out there in a way that is hard to find in a city like Perth, and I was having a sweet time.

With hindsight, I should have been more concerned about the people who were coming to use the place. There were a group of people who were using and abusing Shanti Town, and I didn't want to believe it was happening. I enjoyed getting on the piss with new friends and I was too naïve to see these people didn't care about me or Shanti Town; they were just there to take advantage of my generosity. Three dickheads in particular used to hang around and do burnouts on the public road for the property with one skidding right past the front of the neighbours' houses.

I made myself known to the neighbours and apologised. I said we weren't doing anything illegal and just having a good time on our bikes, and most of them were actually okay with it. Some of them even came over to join us. But after the burnout one of them complained to the City of Armadale council about the shows and the troubles they were bringing. I was contacted by the council, but I still wasn't one for authority and I didn't think it would come to anything. But that one burnout, from one dickhead – a single act of disrespect – was all it took to put us on the radar of the council.

Meanwhile, my friend Michelle called to let me know about a competition she saw in the newspaper. Nitro Circus were touring Australia throughout 2012 and 'Nitro Crew To You' offered for the Nitro Circus gang to visit the winner's town, by giving them ideas on what stunts they could come and do. For people who ran in my circles, the group known as Nitro Circus were gods. They're an American 'action sports collective' who travelled the world doing freestyle motocross, basejumping, and stunts of any kind. They had a TV series, released movies and did live shows, getting paid to do the tricks we loved to do for fun.

The competition was vote-based, and the ideas with the most votes progressed to a top ten, followed by another vote for the winner. I took the time to put a strong entry together and proposed giving the Nitro Circus team a show put on by us instead of the other way around.

We secured a lot of votes, but only finished second in the competition. We were disappointed, but nothing ventured, nothing gained and all that. The winners were a group from Mount Gambier, who proposed Nitro Circus could go there and jump Little Blue Lake, a 40 metre wide sinkhole by the side of a highway. They had the whole town behind their entry. Nitro Circus researched the stunt and found the gap was too wide and the terrain around the sinkhole not suitable for a jump of that size, so instead they were coming to Shanti Town.

The Mount Gambier fans were angry and declared the whole thing rigged, but we were just another ordinary entrant like them. The Nitro Circus staff came to Shanti Town to do a pre-check and inspect the area and everything was sweet, so we had the green light. Having Nitro Circus visit Shanti Town was a dream come true for me, but also a very public reveal of a compound that had previously been a semi-secret. I received calls and text messages from people I hadn't heard from in years wanting to attend the party. I like big parties and so I told everyone to come out, not concerned about a repeat of the idiots from the earlier shows we hosted.

I spoke to my neighbours a month before the event. I explained how we had won the competition and would have the world famous Nitro Circus partying with us for the day. I had my suspicions on which neighbour had called the Council after our last show and I begged and pleaded for him not to report us. I offered him a weekend down in Busselton while the show was on, then dinner at the fancy Coco's in South Perth. I basically said to pick a place for a holiday and I would send him there. He refused my offer for a trip away but promised he would not dob us in to the City of Armadale as long as this was the last show. That was all I needed. "If you don't tell the council we will not have another party," I said, and I meant it.

We charged a small entry fee to come and see Nitro Circus and once again we put on alcohol, food and drinks. The money was put into making the burnout pad bigger so once more there was no profit, but everyone would have one of the best parties of their lives. There was a water slide, bull riding and of course freestyle stunts and burnouts. I tried to keep the party all contained to the back of the property, so the only thing that could be seen from the road was where we parked the cars and the occasional bike flying through the air. Like the rest of the parties, the plan was for this one to just be good fun. There was never anything sinister going on, no fights or aggression and no drugs – just plenty of alcohol. The nearest neighbour was a good 600 or 700 metres away and we were out in the middle of nowhere.

The Nitro Circus team arrived to party on with us and we

Not exactly keeping it quiet, unfortunately a lot of this publiclity would come back to haunt me.

Everyone ready to party at Shanti Town.

turned on a great show for them. We gave them rides in burn-out cars, went crazy on the freestyle and paid tribute to their own antics in our mental way – until the City of Armadale rocked up about an hour into the fun.

The neighbour had gone back on his word and reported us after all. The front gate was locked and my friends were at the gate ticking off names, so all the council officer could see from the road was cars being parked up and a truck and bus associated with the show. I was called over and I explained we were just having a party, advising him that we had notified the neighbours and it would all be over by 5pm. The officer was high on his own bureaucratic power, a real fuckwit, and was not interested in negotiating. "If you don't tell everyone to piss off right now you will be seeing us in court," he spat, flicking a still-smouldering cigarette into the dry grass.

I asked him to give us a break but he could not have cared less; the council was fixing for a fight. "I don't give a shit. I hope you have deep pockets," he said. I returned to the party and got on a microphone to tell everyone what was going on. I explained how the City of Armadale were taking me on, and I could call off the day now and send everyone home or keep it going and take on the council in court. Would everyone support me if I did? Cheers went up, with everyone saying in unison that they had my back, and I felt a surge of pride in what we had achieved at Shanti Town.

The party kept going. Half the Nitro Circus crew left on their bus at 4pm while the other half stayed to party with us, which I took as a sign we were doing something right. From that point on we didn't have any burnouts or freestyle displays, we just got the bonfire burning and let people continue drinking into the night, just like any other party. We were a bunch of guys and girls who wanted to have fun but didn't want to go into the city with all the druggies and violence. We wanted to sit around on a block of land, drink and stay out of harm's way with our bikes.

Two months later I received a letter from the City of Armadale summoning me to court. Well, technically Uncle Phil did, because it was his land, but I wasn't going to leave him holding the baby from my fun. Property inspectors from the Council had been on to the land for an inspection and compiled a list of everything they found wrong. Someone at the council must have really had something against us, because they got us on anything they could find. We were cited for the placement of clean fill for our ramps, which were above a legal height. The sea container was apparently placed illegally and the associated building works (our bar and lean-to) were not approved. They said we had an illegal vehicle wrecking yard there, despite there being only one car on the property – and even that one was still registered. We were charged with illegal storage because of a water tank, an insulation panel and the stunt ramps. They even got us for commercial vehicle parking for what the officer had seen on the day; they didn't miss a trick. But the big charges were for 'commencing of burnout and motorbike sport', as the council lawyers thought we were actually putting on races.

I consulted a lawyer myself and quickly learned it would cost a lot of money to defend the charges in court. The fees just for consultations began to stack up and I thought it was time to draw on the Shanti Town community for support, those people who had cheered me on to keep the party running. I put a post on Facebook and waited for people to get in touch, but instead of cheers and donations I got only silence. Of course everyone had been keen to help when they were full of alcohol and in the middle of a party, but when crunch time came they were nowhere to be found. Hundreds of people used and enjoyed Shanti Town but in the end just five people donated money and four of them had never even been to Shanti Town, they were just good friends – the kind I should have been partying with. It was a big lesson for me on what kind of people to trust, and on the power of the system.

I sought quotes from three different lawyers. Two didn't want anything to do with me and the other said it would be anywhere from $35,000 to $50,000 in fees whether I won or lost. Our case was made difficult by the videos that were uploaded to YouTube and Facebook following not just Nitro Circus but our other events. The council had seen the videos and it gave them the evidence they needed to back up their charges.

After finding out how much lawyers would cost, I started doing my own research and thought we could represent ourselves in court. Before the trial, I made the mistake of trusting the City of Armadale's solicitor, who said I could represent Phil as his agent and explain my side of the story on behalf of Phil.

We got to the trial and I was told I couldn't be Phil's agent, and it was Phil who was going to be on the stand because it was his land. I wasn't the one who was legally responsible, despite my role in everything, and for two days I had to watch the City of Armadale's team present their side. I couldn't say a word as they rolled out the evidence – and they had plenty of it. I was the last person to speak in the trial and I tried to explain my side of things but some of what I said did not line up with what Phil said and the judge didn't like that. Our case was hopeless.

If the maximum penalty for each count we were found guilty of was added up, it equalled $1.6 million and the council was seeking 10% of that. The judge ruled a final fine of $78,850. Believe it or not, the fine was less than I was expecting. I joked with Uncle Phil that at least it wasn't $79,000. He asked the obvious question, "How are you going to pay it, Benny?"

I said I would think of something; I'd work it out like everything else. I sent an email to my closest group of friends, explaining that I did not want any money, I just wanted help in whatever shape it came. From 30 emails I received seven replies. It was a better strike rate than appealing to everyone who had been at the Nitro Circus party, but again I learned who my true friends were. Maybe people thought finding the money would be easy because my family had been wealthy, but all I could do was go to work and pay down the fine. I had made my choices and I had to own up to the consequences.

Here's some tough love if you are going through some kind of bad situation or trauma: once you own the consequences you control them. Remain positive and optimistic for the potential in your future and your ability to control the situation.

I don't ever wish the past could be changed, but I do wish I had thought more about the future during the fun times at

Shanti Town. If I had the knowledge and experience I do now, I don't think I would have been so open to letting anyone and everyone enjoy what we built. I could have kept the compound a secret and still been enjoying it. It was all good to have people who said they were my friends, but when the time came to support the cause, those people weren't there.

Swiss Cheese

It's funny how lots of decisions can eventually align and cause unexpected consequences. I've heard it called the Swiss cheese effect. Imagine that a stack of swiss cheese slices is like a spectrum of safety, with a good result on one side and a bad one on the other. You start on the good side, but each bad decision or risk is like a hole in a slice of cheese; with enough holes (risk) you will see through the stack, and that's when something goes wrong. It's a visual representation of layers of risk prevention.

I had experienced this a year previous, though I didn't realise it at the time. Despite my big quad accident at the Motorcycle and Scooter Show and my later alcohol-fuelled stupidity when I crashed my car, I went out of my way to combine freestyle and booze about a year later. I headed to Lancelin, a beach town north of Perth with flowing sand dunes that were like a playground for riders, where my friends had brought a ramp to use. Jumping from a ramp on to dunes is awesome, because it's really hard to over-jump – which had been my mistake before my accident. Sand is forgiving and jumping is under control provided you know the environment, because the dunes constantly shift and change shape.

I still didn't have my driver's licence, so I hitched a ride to

Lancelin with my friends. On the two hour drive from Perth I knocked down an entire bottle of Jack Daniel's (my first bad decision, and first hole in the cheese) and when we arrived I was so keen to go jumping that I didn't even bother to warm my quad up, I just rode into the ramp and committed (second hole). I hadn't spent any time monitoring the weather conditions before I rode (third hole); I was caught by the wind and landed sideways, the quad's weight coming down on my freshly healed leg. All of the bad decisions had lined up to cause a serious problem – or in the context of our visual metaphor, I'd made it through the slices of Swiss cheese. The nerf bars on the side of the quad crushed my leg and the bones fractured around the existing steel plate. "It's broken, I know it's broken," I said as the boys came to see if I was alright.

I didn't take my riding boot off because I knew the leg would

My friend Colin's helmet-cam captured the aftermath of my crash in the Lancelin sand dunes.

swell, so I just loosened it and poured ice in. We drove out of the dunes and on to the highway for Perth (though we stopped briefly for pizza) and in about 90 minutes I was in the familiar waiting room of Royal Perth Hospital.

In theory, the crash should have just snapped my leg, but within a few weeks I was walking again. The bigger bones in my body healed well and thankfully those were the ones I kept breaking. I did feel bad that my only holidays were coming with a hospital visit attached though.

I begun landscaping full time for myself at the start of 2013, but stunt riding remained a side hustle. One of my freestyle mates, Darren, was preparing a site at Perth Motorplex as part of a Monster Truck show at the end of 2013. Riders would do jumps and tricks to help entertain the crowd during breaks in the event and he wanted to add a quad element. I was invited to the Motorplex to show the organisers what I could do. Maybe I could get a show in front of 10,000 spectators – I'd never had a bigger audience than that.

I had just bought a Suzuki LTR450 as a new freestyle machine. It took some time to get comfortable on the new quad but I was feeling confident enough to use it for the show. I went to look at the site's set up the day before the show to make a few test jumps. They had an Aussie Comp-spec ramp there, which I was very familiar with, and the only problem during my tests was the rear suspension bottoming out. The suspension was still factory original, so it wasn't an unexpected issue. The organisers enjoyed my preview show and asked me to perform the following day. Overnight I changed out the suspension for a brand new spring and was ready for more practice the following morning.

I'd like you to return to that thought about the Swiss cheese effect here, as I have since reflected many times how my decisions on that Saturday morning in November 2013 changed my life. I still didn't have my driver's licence which meant I needed a friend to give me a lift to the Motorplex (first hole in the cheese). I was due to arrive at 9am for practice, but he was two hours late and by the time we arrived at the Motorplex, the site had been changed and the ramp had been moved into an awkward position (second hole). When I hit ramps for the first time at a site, I like to test them at 40 feet apart to get a feel, increasing the distance afterwards to 75 feet. These ramps were set 55 to 60 feet apart. The down ramp was based on a truck, which I had landed on before, but never at a massive gap.

I asked the other guys performing in the show if they could adjust the ramp while I familiarised with the distance. One of the riders got narky about moving the set up and wanted to make a big deal of it; I tried to explain my situation but he wouldn't listen. After some back and forth he was only getting more annoyed. "Fuck it, I will deal with it," I told myself (third hole). My suspension was still new and untested (fourth hole) and I rode around the ramps for a while, trying to get a feel for what speed I needed to make the distance.

I studied the ramp but something felt off and I hesitated. I made 12 test runs when my normal practice routine was to do one or two tests before committing to the jump. That moment right there told me I wasn't ready for this, as much as I wanted to be a part of the show. I finally committed on my 13th run and I hit the ramp with lots of speed as I tried to compensate for the increased distance. I realised I had fucked up almost instantly, and thus with five holes through the cheese I could see all the way through to a bad result. I went up beautifully and was floating through the air but I had left the ramp way too fast, more suited to the full 75 feet I normally jumped. I knew it was going to be a painful experience as gravity took over and brought the ground rushing up to meet me.

The quad missed the ramp and landed flat on the dirt, turning all of the wheel rims into D-shapes. The suspension completely collapsed, the handlebars bent and the engine mounts went through the crankcase, such was the force of the impact. Once the mechanical components had absorbed the blow, it was my turn and I felt my body crumble around me. I could sense every bone individually snapping, especially my legs and wrists. I was first aware of breaking my right calcaneus (heel bone) badly, but in fact it had gone out the back of my foot, right through the Achilles tendon. It was some the most intense pain I have ever felt, like someone was putting a blowtorch to my ankle. My torso fell forward on to a GoPro camera mount hard enough to break my sternum.

I could analyse in my mind which bones were breaking as it happened (that's when you know you have crashed too much). I was pretty sure I had two broken legs, two broken ankles and two broken wrists. I pulled the clutch lever in and rode with my knees gripping the tank, the only way I could get purchase. The boys there all knew the seriousness of the crash and called me an ambulance as they lifted me off the quad and laid me down on the ground. "Fuck, at least I get a holiday now," I thought to myself, flat on my back and in a world of hurt.

After the adrenaline wore off the shock began to set in, an automated physical response to the trauma, and I knew to expect it. I started to get real thirsty and one of the boys handed me a bottle of water, when a security guard wandered over. She said I needed to stop drinking the water because I would have to be operated on.

"If you want, I can tip a little bit of water on my hand and

On the ground at the Motorplex after the big one.

rub it on the inside of your mouth for you so it doesn't get dry," she said. I imagined her wet fingers roaming inside my mouth.

"I don't mean to be rude," I replied. "But I don't when the last time you rubbed your pussy or your ass was."

She looked at me blankly after the awkward conversation, and I guess she was only trying to help, but it seemed disgusting at the time. The ambulance arrived and the paramedics started their work on me, making sure I was stable and checking I had no spinal injuries. They started to take my beautiful Alpine Star Tech 10s boots off and when the left boot came off gently I was hopeful they might not have to be cut open. I had broken my left leg three times in these boots and the right leg twice, yet I was strangely sentimental. I let them try to remove the right boot but it caused agonising pain. For several minutes we pulled and pushed unsuccessfully, but they ended up cutting the right boot off.

My ankles hurt but the rest of my legs weren't bothering me so much, nor the wrists. I was even texting people afterwards saying I was okay. I was given the 'green whistle' (an emergency painkiller and sedative) to try and bring the pain in my ankles down; I can normally keep a lid on my pain but this was hard going and spoke to the seriousness of my injuries. Maybe I'm used to the dosage thanks to my many accidents, or perhaps it was the extent of the damage to my body, but the whistle did nothing for me so the paramedics switched to the more serious painkiller ketamine. Ketamine is a horse tranquiliser, and holy fuck did it take me for a ride. I had hallucinatory conversations in the ambulance as we drove to Royal Perth Hospital and tried to convince the paramedic to take me to Fiona Stanley Hospital, which was still being built. I then invited them to a Mexican restaurant so I could shout them lunch for saving my life. The hallucinations became more bizarre as the trip went on, and I saw four men in white suits standing in front of me. My mate Tim was riding in the ambulance with me and I called out to him for help, wondering what the fuck was going on. I heard a faint reply, almost like a whisper, "Yes, I'm here." When I heard Tim's voice the people in suits disappeared and in their place was a dark tunnel. It felt like I was strapped to the roof of a train and I could see out the end of the tunnel to a big white light. When the ketamine took me to the end of the tunnel, the ambulance opened up around me and I could see the paramedic again.

My mind was not much clearer by the time I arrived at the hospital. The doctors were asking me what happened, trying to get details, but the only thing I could concentrate on in my haze was a beautiful nurse with a Scottish accent. She had all these tattoos, I'm not sure if they were real or imagined, and I could see her body but her face was blurred out, like when they hide someone's identity on a TV show. "Did you know that Scotland has the highest sales of sex toys?" I told her, pouring on as much charm as I could while the painkillers flowed.

I don't remember a great deal from after that, as I was sedated further and sent in for my first operation. A K-wire was needed to hold my busted foot together, a straight piece of metal with a hook on the end that would hopefully convince the bones to fuse back together.

I woke up the next day and started coming to, still under the effects of morphine. Despite the opiates in my system, my mind was more clear than the day before. I realised my leg was in a cast after the surgery but had since swelled up further, pushing my skin into the plaster and causing massive bruising and blisters, just to add to my list of problems. When I was finally coherent enough to speak, the doctors gave me a list of the damage:

- Dislocation of ankle joint
- Fracture of lateral malleolus
- Fracture of navicular scaphoid (foot)
- Fracture of lower end radius with dorsal angulation
- Dislocation of radioulnar joint (distal)
- Fracture of navicular scaphoid (hand)
- Fracture of triquetral bone
- Dislocation of various parts of the wrist
- Fracture of sternum
- Blister of ankle and foot
- Fracture of calcaneus
- Fracture lower tibia and fibula x 2
- Fracture of talus x 2

I had broken so many bones that blood clots became a severe risk. The clots travelled into my lungs and made it difficult to breathe; it felt like someone was standing on my chest. I needed another operation to put a filter inside my main artery to catch the clots before they reached my lungs. Part of that surgery involved a plasma transfusion, which resulted in my whole body getting itchy welts. Pain is one thing but the welts were a horrible kind of torture; so many places on my body were itchy and I couldn't reach them to scratch. During the same operation the doctors bandaged up my left leg and wrist and I was put on a waiting list for further operations. After several more days in the trauma ward being stabilised, I was sent to Bentley Hospital to wait until the next surgery.

I was between the event and the solution, waiting for the next step. This stage was testing for me as my improvement was slow, because they hadn't really fixed me yet, and I realised I needed to change my mindset. I planned activities to occupy my mind and my first objective was toilet independence, which started with getting from the bed to a wheelchair. Requiring a bed pan and someone to wipe my ass was a degrading thing, as necessary as it may have been, and being able to go to the bathroom myself again was a massive boost to my confidence.

Once I could get as far as the bathroom, I was also able to have a shower. When I was stuck in bed I had to settle for a wipe down with a cloth from the nurse, which wasn't nearly as good as the fantasy. Getting to accomplish these basic tasks was like growing from a toddler to an independent child in fast-forward. Technically I wasn't even supposed to be in a wheelchair yet, and I pleaded ignorance when the nurse asked if I was allowed. I knew if she checked my notes she would see I was meant to be in bed but she fortunately turned a blind eye. She could see I wasn't injuring myself any further and she understood the benefits to me mentally. I was still bored, but I stopped the dull nature of my days from affecting me by going for these basic goals.

Mum visited me every day in hospital and helped me out with showering and cleaning, bringing me food and giving me a hand into the wheelchair when I needed. She was positively minded and really wanted to assist, understanding what I wanted from her in hospital. I felt her love and care and noticed the difference in her relationship to me with this injury. When I had cancer, I think she felt helpless, and that left her rudderless in a sea of her own emotions. There was little she could do but watch the nurses administer the chemicals. But when I was laying in hospital with broken limbs, she was able to participate and be involved, and that was important for her. It gave her a purpose and a direct way to help me, which she wanted to do.

I was still distant with Dad, and his visits were tough work. We weren't arguing at least, but we'd exchange pleasantries and not much else. Mum let me know in advance when he planned on visiting to give me time to mentally prepare. One day he walked into my room while Nanna Jean and Mike were visiting; Dad still didn't seem all there. "How are you going, mate?" he said. He was wobbling and swaying, and grabbed one of my broken ankles to give it a hard squeeze. The pain was extreme as his big hand clamped down on my shattered bones.

"What the fuck are you doing?" I yelled at him, and we might have had a blue right there in the hospital room, my four broken limbs and all, were it not for Nan and Mike prudently ushering him out of the room. It was strange looking back, because it seemed like he genuinely cared how I was, but his actions were disconnected from the words.

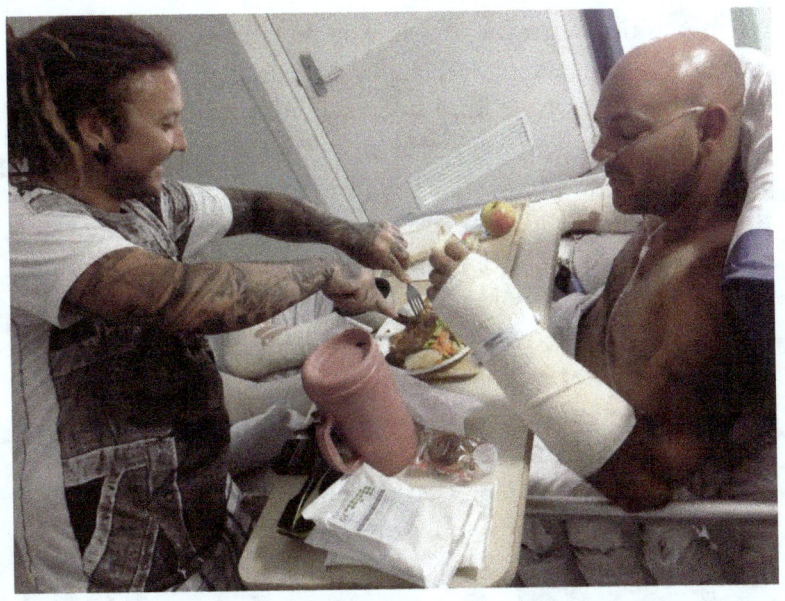

Getting by with a little help from my friends.

My brief stay at Bentley was soon over and I returned to Royal Perth Hospital so the doctors could operate to insert a plate and screws in my left ankle. In total 17 screws were driven into the bone. My right wrist had a plate and screws added as well, while the left wrist was wired up, all in one operation. I always thought twice about public hospitals because I was told when I was younger that they were a poor choice, but I have had more luck in the public hospitals than the private ones if I'm honest. I had many different doctors giving their input on how best to treat me and at one stage I had 30 doctors working on solutions to fix my right ankle alone. What a case I must have been.

Once I had recovered from the operation I was moved to Shenton Park for the rehabilitation process. I had prior experience with the place after my first big accident, and everything was much the same; the nurses even remembered me from the first visit. They had a good laugh at me being back again after having the exact same kind of crash and they took the opportunity to crack a few jokes at my expense. Drawing on my experience, I worked on developing good relationships with the nurses, who sometimes even had their lunch with me. They must have been bored, and tired of some of the more demanding patients, whereas I could crack jokes for them and try to make their days better. Anything I could do to make my environment brighter was helpful to both them and I.

I had to do all I could to stay positive in Shenton Park, because the place had a sad and sorry atmosphere. I understood how people became depressed there because the fucking place looked like a mental asylum from a horror movie; add that most people were recovering from a traumatic event and it was a perfect setting for the blues to set in.

A lot of senior nurses, the 'old boilers' I called them, went to Shenton Park before they retired. They didn't have to do much there as it was a pretty relaxed place where everyone was medically stable. People just needed a hand getting into wheelchairs, showering and moving to the gym for their physiotherapy. The boilers weren't interested in making the most of their career twilight, or growing their experiences, and I thought this created a negative influence. Thankfully the young nurses were vibrant and added colour to the place; positive people make all the difference in a recovery.

I was lucky in a sense, because my injuries were self inflicted, which made it easier to own my recovery. No matter what injury I get on a bike it will always be 100% my fault, because I am the one who chooses to twist the throttle. Cancer was a very different mental battle. I was able bodied, but rendered useless by the chemotherapy – and it was not my fault, my number just came up. I imagine it was the same for people who had road accidents where they were the innocent party. Ownership of the problem gave me power in the rehabilitation stage.

I see young fellas get involved in action sports, who then cry wolf about how bad things are when they get injured. If they're scared of pain, why jump a bike? It's not a case of if, but when they will crash. People love the glory but can't cope with the other side of the sport, which is broken bones, and they will let themselves spiral into self pity. A negative mind is a hindrance to recovery and by making a choice to participate in a risky sport, people also need to choose to accept the consequences of the risk. It all comes back to owning your choices.

I spent two weeks in Shenton Park, but like my first time I could do little to speed my physical recovery. My broken bones were still healing, so the nurses were mainly assessing if I could use a wheelchair and keeping an eye on the blood clots. After seeing me roll speed trials on the paths around the hospital, they felt confident enough to release me. It was December 13, 2013, just under five weeks since my accident.

After being released from hospital I went to my favourite pub, The Gate. I gorged on the tasty food and alcohol, which I hadn't been allowed in hospital, and quickly got drunk. Being December, a lot of staff Christmas parties were taking place, and some guy was dancing on a chair. He had a bit of a circle going on with people clapping around him and I wanted to join in the fun. Full of Dutch courage, I rolled into the circle with my wheelchair and did a wheelie, showing off my moves before I lost my balance and flipped straight out the back of it like a clown, leaving everyone laughing and cheering. They put me back in the wheelchair and off I rolled again.

I stayed at my Uncle Phil's while I was recovering because I had a lot of appointments to attend back at the hospital. Many of my friends came to say hello and take me on outings and I was grateful to be busy. Every two weeks I went in for an update on my progress; most of my bones were healing but the right ankle was showing no improvement. Doctors were waiting for the bone to grow and turn into a mass that would fuse itself together. That meant I would have virtually no ankle movement and I thought it was a bad idea, but I wasn't a doctor.

Shortly before Christmas I picked up my Suzuki quad, which had been repaired from the accident. I was keen to ride and I organised a trip to Exmouth with some mates. I thought some fishing and some hooning on the quad would test how bad my injuries were and let me measure my recovery so far.

Before we went for our trip I met a girl, and we hit it off. We were in the early days of seeing each other but I suggested she should come to Exmouth for the getaway. I still didn't have my licence back and I was trying to behave myself, so it helped that she could do the driving. I felt like she was hot and cold on me, but figured she wouldn't go all the way to Exmouth if she wasn't interested. We made it up to our accommodation no worries and things seemed pleasant, but we had an argument when I saw messages she was sending to another guy. We had a big fight and I told her to fuck off on the next plane home; I was really pissed. For some reason, I took out a lot of frustration from my accident on her, using the messages as a catalyst. It was one of the few times in my recovery where my emotions boiled over. It certainly wasn't fair on her to unleash all of my pent up feelings, and I was regretful afterwards. I sent her flowers, but we didn't speak after that – and I can't blame her really.

Even though I was disabled I was still determined to imitate an able-bodied lifestyle. Before I was injured I had signed up for the Australian International Billfish Tournament fishing competition. This involved deep sea fishing for three days on my friend Shane Stephen's boat, even though I had no idea if I could swim in a moon boot and plaster cast. I didn't want to find out how deep the water was by walking off the back of the boat, as my Uncle Steve had once suggested.

Big game fishing is a huge physical challenge. You're chasing the pelagic species like sailfish and marlin, and some of these fish weigh hundreds of pounds. They're pure muscle and dash through the water at tremendous speeds when hunting; up to 100kph. I had two broken arms and two broken legs but I was determined to fight for the fish. I wore my arm casts to wind them in and wedged myself into the back corner of the boat, levering up and down on the fishing rod. My buddy Paul Murdoch was also there to help with everything, even holding on to me when I was taking a leak off the back of the boat so I didn't

Paul Murdoch and I with one of the sailfish I caught with two broken arms and two broken legs.

fall into the deep blue water.

We had a brilliant time, with one of our three sailfish catches winning the division and another couple of marlin, but by the end of our time on the boat my right leg was severely swollen and I knew something wasn't right. Still feeling frustrated at the situation with my lady friend and wanting to find out what was wrong with my leg, I thought, "Fuck it." I decided to drive home without a licence, or an able body for that matter. One of my mates drove me past Exmouth Airport so I could avoid the worst of the police presence in the town and then I was on my own. I didn't have much feeling in my right leg so I wedged my foot between the accelerator pedal and the firewall. Somehow I drove through the bigger towns of Carnarvon and Geraldton without police attention and continued through the night, avoiding the hundreds of kangaroos and other wildlife that crowd the road after dark. I arrived back in Perth at 5am after leaving Exmouth at 5pm. I've done many stupid, dangerous things and that trip in the car was up there. I was annoyed that my leg was still not getting better and I took out my frustration on the drive.

It strikes me now how recent that was, and how much I have changed since.

Chopped

After returning to Perth, I went straight to hospital for a check up where the doctors told me the K-wires in my right foot were snapping. The guilty thought materialised that it could have been a result of my adventures in Exmouth, but the doctors told me the bone was simply not fusing correctly after three months. A bone can heal to 80% strength in six weeks, but there had been zero bone growth in my ankle since November. The doctors started to take interest in me again.

A nurse referred me to Professor Rene Zellweger, the doctor who helped me through my first accident. He remembered me from then and I thought his no-bull attitude would be helpful once again. The Professor checked out my foot and proposed he could take a sample of bone out, grow it in a lab and then return it to the ankle in the hope it would heal itself. But even if the process worked I would still have restricted flexibility so it wasn't much of an improvement, in my mind.

He then asked, almost as an aside, if I had considered amputation. The truth was I had, especially after talking with my mate Rod Angwin, who was an amputee. The Professor thought he had given me the worst case scenario, but the more we discussed amputation the more it seemed like the best option. I returned to speak with him another two times as we weighed the pros and cons of giving my leg the chop from the knee down. My foot was already discoloured from lost circulation and when I walked it felt squishy, like I was treading on soft soap all the time. Professor Zellweger explained that if the foot didn't heal, it would be deemed a loss of foot regardless, as nothing more could be done in surgery to return it to health.

The recovery time for an amputation was relatively quick for a healthy person and the Professor told me I could be back on my feet (or foot I suppose) within six weeks. The decision seemed obvious to me and I couldn't see a down side in my sit-

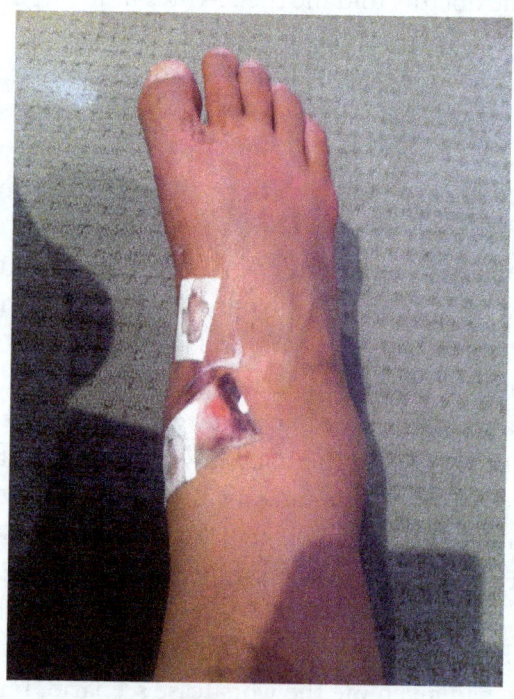

Years of accidents and surgery had taken their toll on my foot.

uation, once I got past the mental block of losing a part of my body, something I was no stranger to. The Professor had been sending me home after each appointment to contemplate the choice but I already had my mind made up. I certainly didn't want to be stuck with a Gumby foot for the rest of my life, half healed and creating more issues. More time to consider an amputation only gave me more confidence in the choice.

I didn't talk the amputation over with anyone besides the Professor; I owned the decision. My new girlfriend noticed how much I was in and out of hospital, and I eventually explained the reason to her. I couldn't spend my days carrying a dead foot around and amputation solved an impediment instead of creating one.

Once I told Professor Zellweger I wanted to go ahead with the amputation, he said I was the perfect candidate for the operation. He understood that I was confident about the decision and he believed owning my own business meant I was motivated for recovery. I respected him a lot, especially when he told me I would be able to get back on a bike and ride again. I felt a lot of doctors in hospital looked down at me when I was in there for a bike accident, like somehow I was taking the place of someone who deserved to be in the bed more than me. But Professor Zellweger was down to earth and understood my wild life wasn't going to change.

When I was first in hospital after the Motorplex accident, my bed was next to a man who lost his leg in an accident of his own. In the haze of my post-surgery meds, I gazed at his prosthetic limb, a scary looking remnant from the 1960s made of old brown, old leather. He had boating moccasins on to complete the look and the leg frightened the fuck out of me; it looked like an antique of medicine that belonged in a museum.

I imagined losing my own leg at the time and now it was about to happen for real.

I can't deny I had a mental advantage over other amputees; I wasn't waking up from an accident and finding out I didn't have a leg anymore. When I talk about owning the choice, and the consequences, I understand how difficult that can be when you don't get a say in the first place. But I think we are all capable of structuring our thoughts so that we own a situation, even one not of our creation. If you can own a problem you have control, and then you have power.

I had three weeks to wait from the time I made the decision to amputate until the operation, and I vowed I wasn't going to miss that leg. You might be looking at your own leg right now, imagining what it would feel like to know you were headed for an amputation, but chances are you have a great leg. Imagine instead your leg was in pain with every step, slowly dying and preventing you from leading the life you loved – imagine relief instead of loss. The solution seemed extreme, but an amputation would restore function for me where I had none.

I psyched myself up for the chop, scheduled for May 5, 2014. I went into the hospital with Mum, only for them to announce my operation had been pushed back a day, I couldn't believe it! I had to get pumped up again the next morning and thankfully this time I was taken to the anaesthetist where I expected to be knocked out very shortly. But I got another surprise when he said he would not put me to sleep. "You're not?" I questioned.

The anaesthetist said he wasn't going to perform any medical procedures because the doctor doing the operation, Professor Zellweger, had not done the proper research and I was not on the right medication. The medication he was talking about was antidepressants and they weren't to aid in the physical recovery, only in the mental outlook of patients post-operation. My operation had a big difference however – I was choosing to be amputated. He started going on about how I needed the proper counselling and I had to go away and come back in a month. I couldn't believe what he was saying, why was this suddenly such a big deal? My blood pressure was skyrocketing right before going into major surgery.

"I'm here for a reason," I said. "I have been through so much shit with this leg and you need to talk with the doctor right now because you are just here to put me to sleep."

Professor Zellweger overheard the commotion as our voices raised. He came into the room and asked what the issue was, and the anaesthetist told him the same thing – big mistake. The Professor wasn't just a good doctor, he was also the head of trauma for the entire hospital and nobody messed around with him. He dragged the anaesthetist out of the room and the nurses and I listened as Professor Zellweger gave hell next door, yelling and screaming. He really got stuck into the guy.

"You don't argue with Zellweger," one of the nurses whispered.

The anaesthetist returned to the room with his tail between his legs and apologised. "I will be putting you to sleep today, Mr Stevens," he said. After that he was as good as gold, but I thought his decision to make a stand as I was being wheeled into theatre was surreal.

Now I had the green light, and the assembled doctors and nurses started by giving me an epidural and ketamine, paralysing my lower half. As we moved closer to the operation I tried to barter with the nurses to keep the steel plates from my leg as a souvenir; they laughed me off and told me it would be too risky. As we moved under the lights, the thin sheet over me parted and I had a good last look at the bottom of my right leg.

"Goodbye, leg," I said. And I was out of it.

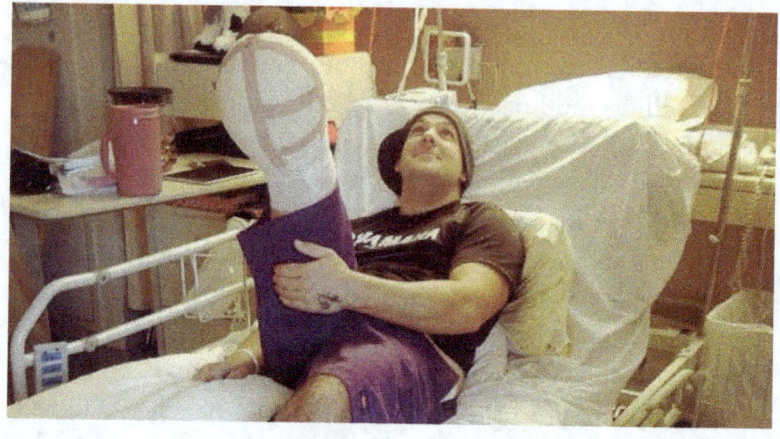

Proper 'legless' for the first time.

Removing the leg was surprisingly simple, and the operation took a grand total of 45 minutes. The doctors cut the skin and muscle on each side of the leg, then they used a saw to cut through the tibia and fibula bones. The skin from the lower part of the leg was used as a flap that they folded over the wound and stitched up.

I woke after the operation and looked down my body to see a thick ball of bandages where the bottom of my right leg had been. I lifted it up and I noticed how light it felt. "No turning back now," I thought.

I was on a cocktail of painkillers after surgery, and the morphine kept me awake for the next two nights. It wasn't so bad as I laid in bed listening to my music or playing games on an iPad. The only thing that bothered me was the old bloke in the bed next to mine, who turned on his TV with the volume so loud I could hear it past my headphones; I wondered if he had trouble sleeping too.

In the early stages of my recovery, each day felt like the last.

Tubes on each side of my right leg sucked the blood from the bottom of the stump, and I couldn't move around a great deal.

In one of the days after my operation I had ten minutes where I felt my heart sink, the closest I had felt to regret. I took a deep breath when I looked at my leg. "This is going to be a fucking mission," I thought. I realised the damage I would do to my mind if I second guessed myself now, and I snapped myself out of the negativity and tried to reset my perspective. I'd been through worse and I was capable of getting through this too. For all the trials of life I had experienced, that was my reward; I had experience in being dealt a bad card and I told myself to be positive. I understood the nature of my lifestyle and that my choices had consequences.

Three days after my operation my friends told me they had a surprise lined up for me. I had some suspicions, but it really brightened me up and I figured whatever it was, I had better ease up on the painkillers so I could remember.

I couldn't believe it when the Nitro Circus crew came into my room! They were in town for a show and after our efforts at Shanti Town they wanted to drop by and check up on me. Aaron 'Wheelz' Fotheringham, Streetbike Tommy, Jolene, Clinton Moore, they were all my heroes and it was awesome for them to take time out of their busy schedules to visit. We had a fun time talking about stunts and crashes and I was on a high long after they left the hospital.

Without the morphine in my system I finally felt tired enough to sleep. Night fell and I was trying to get some shut-eye, when old mate in the bed next to mine turned his TV up loud again. He was listening to Double J, with rap and hip-hop blaring from the speakers. With the cloud of painkillers no longer fogging my brain I was more alert to my surroundings,

A visit from the Nitro Circus gang raised my spirits.

and I started listening more closely. I could hear his bed being lowered down, screeching in the night. "Ohhhhh, Pedro," I heard him say. I could hear this buzzing sound starting up, soft then loud, and then moaning. Bzzzzzzzz.

"Get fucked," I thought to myself.

I pressed the call button for the nurse, who arrived and asked me what I needed. I didn't want to say it out loud in case the old man overheard, because I was never sure if someone was mentally stable in hospital. I took a piece of paper and wrote a note:

> *The old guy next to me is fucking himself with a vibrator.*

The nurse went wide eyed and put her hand over her mouth as she started laughing. She went outside to tell the other nurses and I heard giggling in the hallway before she returned and offered some earplugs. I took my notepad again:

This is fucked. You need to sort this out. I need to be in another room.

She again went out of the room. We negotiated back and forth for four hours as I tried to get moved to another room. The nurse then came back and whispered to me that no other rooms were available and I would have to deal with it.

"If you don't get me out of this room, the next person to come and see me will beat the fuck out of this guy," I told the nurses.

Here I was recovering from my leg getting chopped off and I'm listening to an old man pleasuring himself with 'Pedro'; eventually I couldn't stand it anymore. "Bugger this, I don't need to be listening to this shit," I thought. Next to my bed was a jug of water, which I wanted to douse him with. The nurses saw and tackled me before I could ditch the water, and it was quite the scene developing.

This time one of the nurses opened the curtain next to his bed, and there was old mate with his legs up in the air and his hand between his cheeks holding a sex toy. He was recovering from back surgery but it didn't appear to have affected his flexibility, and his legs dropped to the bed with a thud as he realised he had been discovered. "I am doing nothing, nothing!" he said. The vibrator was still buzzing away up his ass for all to hear.

I felt a touch bad later on because I thought maybe the old man had dementia. But I'd overheard conversations he had with his children about money and land where he seemed to have mental clarity, and his plan to mask the sound of the vibrator was too well thought out. Maybe he was just a deviant, but the whole incident actually resulted in a full blown investigation at the hospital and became a running joke with the nurses for months afterwards, who asked me if I had heard 'Pedro' lately. The good news was I got a single room after the incident. Starting the day with Nitro Circus and finishing listening to an old guy getting himself off with a vibrator, what a life.

My leg had soon improved enough for the nurses to take out the tubes inserted at the stump after the operation. Professor Zellweger came by and asked me how I was going.

"Apart from old pricks with vibrators, pretty good," I said.

He had brought a trainee in with him so she could learn how this was done. He explained to her to tell me to take a deep breath and then to rip the tube out in one quick pull. Unfortunately she didn't listen and when I finished with the breath she started to pull the tube out excruciatingly slowly; I rank it as the second worst pain I have ever felt after my burns as a kid. I yelled in agony and the Professor urged her to go quicker, until he was forced to take over and ripped out one tube, then the other in swift movements. My heart was pounding and I was shaking from the pain as the nurse apologised; I think she was more traumatised than I was.

Professor Zellweger decided my recovery had reached the point of rehabilitation and said it was time to go to Shenton Park (my third stay for those counting). The stump was extremely sensitive because the bone sat right underneath the skin, and any time I knocked it I felt 'pins and needles'. The nurses made me a cute little stump cover and over time the stump became less sensitive as the nerves and tissue adapted.

I was serious about my recovery and I decided I wanted to beat Professor Zellweger's estimate of six weeks from operation to walking out of the hospital. From the moment I arrived at Shenton Park I was in the gym twice a day, exercising my body to keep my strength up. The nurses worked on reducing the size of my stump by using a suction machine to remove any fluid and blood collecting inside. They needed the size to be as close as possible to my final recovery so I could have the correct socket for my prosthetic leg.

I aimed to enjoy rehabilitation where I could. I met the late John Day, a West Aussie speedway legend who had also just had a leg removed, and the Perth Motorplex chaplain Terry Dorrington regularly joined me for coffee and a catch up. He was there for me a lot in my recovery and we had good talks about life.

I liked to watch people at Shenton Park and I tried to pick the patients who were going to be successful and the ones who were going to struggle, observing the patterns in their behaviour and learning lessons for myself. One thing I noticed was how some people became addicted to painkillers, always demanding more. Sometimes they faked pain like my old mate Clem from the first visit to Shenton Park. Nurses deal with humans every day of their working life and they know the games their patients get up to; they're better at reading people than almost anyone else I believe.

Soon the nurses were happy for me to be sized up for a socket to get my new prosthetic leg. I did some initial fittings where I had a chance to put a leg on and stand up in it, keeping my balance for a while before sitting down. It was sore, but after we did a couple of standing exercises I wanted to try for the next goal. I rolled my wheelchair over to a set of parallel bars where I could balance while I learned to walk again. There I took my first steps with the assistance of the orthotics specialists, the first time I had moved without wheels in weeks. This is usually the part of the story where you would expect me to tell you about all my emotions flooding in as I took steps again, but the only prize I was interested in was complete recovery and becoming as close to a physically normal human being as you can with an artificial leg. Professor Zellweger had said amputation would be perfect for me and I was determined to prove it.

Once I had the first steps under my belt I lost interest in working out my upper body and I focused on increasing how many steps I could make at a time. My competitive nature drove me to better my count each day and within a week I could walk through the parallel bars without being assisted or needing to use the rails. I was soon able to start walking around the actual gymnasium itself, leaving the wheelchair behind, and within two weeks I could walk outside of the gym on a 100 metre exercise track. There I was pleased to discover a small whiteboard that had some walking records listed, with the goal to see how many metres could be walked in six minutes. Having an actual number to beat was an extremely good motivator for me and the nurses let me attempt a record. I managed 200 metres in six minutes, breaking the previous amputee record of 150 metres, and each day I added more steps and speed. By the time I was due to leave Shenton Park, the physiotherapists couldn't even keep up with their measuring wheel while I power walked.

On June 19, 2014, I was given the okay to leave Shenton Park, six weeks and two days after my operation; Professor Zellweger's prediction had been almost perfect and I wondered if he gave me the target to motivate me.

Excited to be home, my heart sank when I opened the door and realised my house had been broken into on the same day I had been released from hospital. Some asshole had been right through the place and stolen the TVs and other bits and pieces, not so happy days!

Though I had been able to use the prosthetic at Shenton Park, it was a couple of weeks until I received my leg to use at home. Life was back to normal surprisingly quickly once I had my new leg. Amputation was a shortcut to recovery and as my leg adapted to the prosthetic I was feeling more able-bodied by the day. Sometimes at the start I had to think through how to change my habits or how I could get from place to place, like going from the kitchen to the lounge room, but my thoughts were practical and I didn't dwell on the negatives.

Anything around the house was pretty mundane stuff if I'm honest. One night I got out of bed to get some chocolate from the fridge when I had a thought flash through my mind: what would happen if a burglar returned to my house? I might look like the Black Knight from Monty Python's Holy Grail trying to fight him off with a stump. I used a positive mind to help me, because what I could or couldn't do was directly related to what I *believed* I could or couldn't do.

Some things were definitely harder, like going for a swim. I'd never been one for going swimming at the beach anyway – I didn't want a shark to take my other leg. There were moments I thought I still had a foot, like when my dogs Abel and Gizmo were fighting. I got up to give them a mouthful, stepping where I thought I still had a foot and instead falling on to my stump. I grimaced on the floor as the pain pulsed from the end of the shortened leg. For a moment I thought I had put a leg bone straight through the skin.

That sounds dramatic but in reality it was a very small hurdle to overcome, it feels wrong even calling it a hurdle. I'm not going to say having a leg chopped off was the easiest thing to do, but it will not hold you back in life. Sometimes I've gone to untie my shoelaces at the end of the day, before remembering I don't have to take my shoe off, only the leg. I just forget I don't have a leg. I might fit under a definition of physical disability but I have chosen not to let that define my life. My friends don't see me any differently since the amputation because I continued my extreme lifestyle.

Once my stump had toughened I wanted to test it out and I decided on another fishing charter in Exmouth, about four months after my operation. This was going to be a 'Welcome Back Benny' party.

I still had no licence and a missing leg forced me to avoid driving, at last. My mate Fingers decided to drive in my Hilux ute and our first stop was The Gate pub to wait for the convoy of cars ready to get on the road. We didn't end up leaving until five hours later and we only got about 90 minutes out of Perth before I needed my first spew stop.

One of the advantages of being a passenger was that I could knock down cans of Jack Daniel's along the drive, but with every can I needed to take a leak. I had my pocket knife with me so I put a hole in a can and relieved myself as we were still driving and when I finished I wound down the window and threw the empty behind our car, all over my friend Barnesy's car behind us. When we stopped driving for a rest in Geraldton, Barnesy was confused rather than angry. "Why were you guys throwing full cans of Jack Daniel's out on the drive? You're just wasting drinks," he said, with no idea his car was getting covered in piss.

We drove through the night on a good old road trip, and arrived at Exmouth at 7am. When we arrived I went straight to sleep, cradling my fake leg in my arms because I knew the boys were planning to fuck with it. Later in the day we took Uncle Steve's boat Blue Horizon on an eight-hour ride to the Montebello Islands, where we had a great time and even caught a sailfish. I was benchmarking my leg against what it had been like when I last went fishing, and it was holding up. The prosthetic felt better than my broken, non-healing foot, which was exactly what I wanted. As we returned for shore I sat down on the deck and thought I would showboat by taking off my leg and filling it with cider to skol down. After I finished I jumped up to celebrate and again forgot I only had one leg, crashing into the bottom of the boat and landing in a box of fishing gear. Better than tumbling off the side into the water!

We were having a blast and everyone was in fine form on their jokes and pranks. My mate Fingers was drinking for most of the boat ride and getting really messed up. He dropped his phone off the side of the boat looking at a shark, then lost his keys when he dived in to retrieve the phone. We cut his fishing line when he wasn't looking and waited to see how long it would take him to notice. When we got back to dry land he sounded like he was dying, and he gave his wallet to another one of my friend Eppo to look after. He kept me awake much of the night with his groaning and he looked like death warmed up in the morning.

I had warned the boys the night before that we had mud-crabbing planned and they shouldn't get too fucked up, but Fingers had got greedy and was out of action for the day. I went to where the air conditioning controllers were and put them up as high as they could go, then locked the door to the room with the controller as I was leaving. Fingers slept off his morning in a stinking hot house which we thought was another great prank and served him right for getting so messy. When we returned, Fingers said he was actually feeling better, though he mentioned he had been sweating a lot and couldn't find his wallet. We told him no one had it and that it must have been stolen, and Fingers spat the dummy. I said he should cancel his cards, so he called his missus, then called the bank and cancelled the lot. Everyone was laughing as he made the calls and about ten minutes after he was finished, Eppo walked over and said, "Are you missing this?" Poor Fingers just about melted down when he realised the prank.

I had a great time away with my friends and the performance of the leg increased my confidence in my decision. I had few doubts I was doing the right thing, but now I had the evidence to prove it.

Fuel for Thought - III

People who didn't meet me until after my amputation find it hard to believe I haven't changed, but I have made a conscious decision not to let it affect me. Every amputee has their own pathway and sometimes their trauma is so bad they can't confront what caused it, like motorcycle riders who can't even look at a bike again. My past experiences and challenges allowed my mind to accept the way my life was, and for that I saw myself as lucky. I don't believe my story is inspiring or even special when I see what other people achieve in their lives, and frankly the amputation was a walk in the park compared to cancer. So long as you can find a way to own the problem, whether that is accepting your choice or knowing that life has hard times, you can take the power back.

I owned the fact that every single time I climb on to a motorcycle it could be the last time I ride in my life. I am the one who chooses to take that risk. How can I be pissed off and angry with myself when that is a choice I made? I am the one who makes the choice so I am the one who deals with the consequences.

The fact I am missing half a leg does not matter, the only thing that matters is what I will do to in the future to manage that fact. I used the same mindset to get through cancer: the problems we are faced with do not change, only our response to them matters. This might not work for everyone, but I can only give the formula that works for me, do with it what you will.

Nitro

A lot of amputees enjoy a second lease on life and start running marathons, climbing mountains or lifting weights. I wanted to go back to what I always loved, which was riding fast vehicles. Missing half a leg, I knew I couldn't do freestyle stunts any more, at least not at the pro level like I wanted. But I did not want to focus on the things I couldn't do; I needed to find something extreme that I could do. I wanted to still fight to be the best, even with the impediment of my amputation.

When I was in hospital after getting the chop, my very good friend Clint looked after me a lot. He was always bringing me good food and things would have been a lot harder without his support. Clint and I were having lunch and he asked what my plans were going to be after I had recovered.

"I want to be the world's quickest and fastest amputee," I said.

"How are you going to do that?" Clint replied.

"A Nitro Harley."

"Mate, you are a fucking dickhead."

Despite Clint's concerns, he said he would be there to help me out with the bike no matter what. Setting myself the goal of riding a motorcycle that could scare even the biggest blokes was a great boost for my mental health while I was in hospital. Instead of all my attention being focused on just losing a leg, I was preoccupied with getting a Nitro Harley. Uncle Kim had sold his own bike to a friend and it had only been raced sporadically since; I figured having a bike we already knew inside out would be a great head start. The new goal setting empowered me with a deep sense of purpose, putting the amputation behind me.

I got the new owner's number and started to pester him about selling it. He wanted to turn it into a dedicated dirt drags bike (an even more insane type of drag racing where guys race on a straight dirt track), but I was persistent. Kim even gave him a call and went into bat for me, telling the owners how he would love to have the bike back in the family. Eventually the pester power worked and we figured out a deal to bring the old girl back home. When we went to collect the bike and I hobbled

Uncle Kim's Nitro Harley coming back to the family.

into the owner's shed on one leg, he must have thought I was crazy, because even riders with two legs can struggle to control these big, heavy bikes.

After we trucked the bike back home we noticed blood all over it; the belt drive, fairing and brakes all had spatters of dark red. We found out the last time the bike had been ridden at the track it had been in a scrape with the safety barriers next to the track, and the rider lost a finger as a result. I'd already lost a leg, so I suppose losing a finger would just be a flesh wound.

I had a feeling of excitement just looking at the high horsepower machine resting peacefully in my shed. It was my goal to ride one of these nitro bikes and we had accomplished the first step towards that target. We left the motorcycle sitting for about a month before we started the engine to make sure everything ran, and then we commenced pulling apart every component to do some fine checks. We spent some time going over the bike and updating some of the equipment to Australian National Drag Racing Association standards. We repaired a crack in the chassis where the chain had been rubbing, went through the electrics and put a new front end on too. We were learning as we went but had some good people giving us advice, and Kim still knew the bike like the back of his hand.

The rebuild was soon complete and I set a date to put some nitro through the engine's veins again. Clint was there to take his promised place on the crew, joined by his friend Brian. My buddy Aaron Deery had some experience with Nitro Harleys, so he visited to help us through the start-up procedure and make sure everything was in working order. Nitro fuel produces incredible amounts of horsepower because of its chemical composition. Unlike normal petrol, nitro carries an oxygen molecule which allows for a greater volume of fuel to be burned. But nitro also has the capacity to blow the cylinder head right off the motor because it will explode when compressed. This can occur if the motor loses spark on a run, but the engines are especially dangerous after they have been turned off. A small amount of nitro left puddled in the cylinders can explode under pressure, even if the motor is just being turned over by hand. Safety is paramount and there are no shortcuts. Aaron helped drum into me the importance of religiously working to a procedure. We were all very green to nitro.

I was eager to see the results of our rebuild and I was confident we had assembled the motor correctly, but I didn't know for sure until I heard the beautiful sound of the v-twin firing. Aaron commenced the start-up with methanol fuel and once the motor was firing he switched to the nitro. The deep pops of each combustion cycle were like music to my ears. Aaron had me climb aboard the bike so I could feel it running underneath me, alive for the first time. The sound demanded my attention, the vibrations shook my whole body, and my nose burned from the nitro fumes. I struggled to see through teary eyes, not from emotion but the yellow-tinged nitric acid exhaust that hung in the air. This machine consumed my senses in a way that made me forget about cancer, my leg or anything else life could throw at me.

With the test start successful, I planned a second test together with my drag racing friend Jon Ferguson. He had a big shed built on a concrete pad, which was the closest we could get to simulating the concrete start line of Perth Motorplex. I treated the day in his shed like a race event, becoming familiar with everything the team and I had to do to the bike before we headed to the track. I was prepared to take all the time in the world to make sure our routine was right, but when it came to being in the seat I wanted to go big and make sure I could handle this thing. I did a huge burnout, leaving the shed filled with white rubber smoke. Though I grew up doing burnouts just for fun, a burnout is essential to the pre-race routine for a Nitro Harley, warming and cleaning the big rear tyre. I've ridden a lot of bikes, but this machine was on the next level; I had 1000 horsepower on tap just by twisting my wrist. What an amazing experience it was to feel every revolution of the motor go through my body, absolutely fucking insane is the only way to describe it.

After the burnout we cleared the engine of nitro and simulated the maintenance required between rounds of racing. I was already excited to be doing another burnout but I wasn't just being a hoon; doing skids was helping me gain a feeling for the bike so I would know what to expect when I finally hit the throttle on the track. I had bravado on my side, but until I was actually in the seat and holding the throttle open, I had no idea if my leg was going to impede my riding. As I practiced burnouts, with smoke billowing from the tyre, I found I could move the bike with my hips and control its attitude. It might be overpowered, ill handling and heavy but it was still just a motorbike; I wasn't going to get this far and give up. As long as I could keep the bike upright I believed I could ride it.

Going racing again was feeling real and I couldn't wait for my first event, but first I had a hurdle to clear. The Australian National Drag Racing Association wanted me to ride in the Modified Bike class before I started licensing on the Nitro Harley. Modified Bike is an entry level class, but very different to riding a Nitro Harley, and the two don't really relate. It's like riding a horse and then trying to ride an elephant; they're the same principle but completely different in practice.

I wanted to follow the rules and be a good boy so I bought a Modified Bike, but I found the seating position awkward because I couldn't bend my leg enough to get my foot on the peg. The Nitro Harley was actually easier to sit on and control because it had a lay down riding position where I was stretched across the top of the chassis with my legs stretched out. I debated the issue with ANDRA and Perth Motorplex's drag racing manager Ray Treasure went into bat for me, because he had seen me driving the Top Doorslammer just under a decade earlier and knew I could control a high speed vehicle. ANDRA relented on the Modified Bike idea but still made me get an entry level drag racing licence first in a Holden Maloo ute doing 13.6 seconds on the quarter mile, about twice as long as the Nitro Harley would take with half the speed. I was told I was being a pain in the ass, and perhaps my confidence going into this new situation came across as cockiness. I wasn't being arrogant, I just think everybody knew it was a meaningless hoop to jump through.

I was ready to make my first runs on December 28, 2014 – six months after my amputation. I had my pit crew assembled and they were eager to move out of the shed and on to the track. They were mostly fresh to drag racing, so my buddy Aaron was back to give us a hand and teach the crew what to do on race day.

Many people talk about the nerves they have before racing. As I stared down the drag strip before my first pass, I was at peace. Doing those few burnouts in the shed gave me confidence in the way the bike felt when the motor was running, how the controls were laid out and what the procedures were for getting to the start line. My own decisions had brought me to this point and I owned all the emotions I felt as the adrenaline kicked in. In a few minutes I would have ridden a Nitro Harley for the first time, and the only thing left to do was take each step after the next.

We started the bike up and I felt the rumble of each nitro

Learning to ride a 1000 horsepower motorcycle.

burning revolution from the motor hitting me in the chest. Aaron helped guide me into a puddle of water to begin the burnout and I cracked open the throttle. I wanted to smoke out the place with a giant burnout, but it was a bit shit if I'm honest! The crew made some final checks and Aaron brought me forward to the start line. The lights on the top of the Christmas tree (drag racing starting lights) glowed to let me know I was perfectly lined up and ready for my run. Three amber countdown lights flashed and then the green.

I smacked the throttle wide open and the bike took off, squatting down on the tyre. I held the power on for just a second, as far as I was allowed to go on my first ride, but it was already everything I had imagined and more. As I backed off the throttle and rolled down the rest of the track I had the biggest smile under my helmet. I was so pleased because it felt just as insane as I wanted it to be!

The experience felt so vivid. Driving Dad's drag car had let me experience high speeds over 300kph, but when I rode fast motorcycles I was so much more aware of everything around me. No rollcage protected me, no carbon fibre body blocked my senses, and I felt vulnerable – in a good way. It really does take balls to ride these things, or one in my case.

When I climbed off the bike after the run I felt my confidence lifting. Some people had suggested to me that riding a Nitro Harley with one leg was not prudent, but even the very short first pass showed I could control the bike and that my leg was not going to be a major impediment.

To get my drag racing licence signed off I had to progress further and further down track each time, demonstrating that I could control the bike and that I was aware of where I was positioned on the track. The more runs I did, the more my brain comprehended what was happening.

Initially we struggled to get the bike to make full power. When a Nitro Harley doesn't make power it can become dangerous, because the chassis is designed to operate correctly at an acceleration maximum. The engine needs to be on full throttle, with the bike balanced on the rear wheel and the wheelie bars down (the frame that hangs out the back of the bike), while the front wheel hangs in the air for the first half of the track, then drops to the ground before the finish line. If you're riding on low power with the front wheel on the ground early, or getting on and off the throttle, the bikes tend to go whichever direction they want and even an experienced rider will struggle to correct the path.

My bike had a lean-out system that was designed to take fuel away from the tune up in the later stages of a run, and we couldn't figure out why it wasn't operating correctly. This meant we were constantly dropping cylinders and I was losing half of my power, so I was stuck at the half track stage of my licensing. Aaron devised a workaround, figuring out a way to make the lean-outs operate, and we finally made a full pass with a time of 8.00 seconds – good enough to have my licence signed off. The Australian record for a Nitro Harley was 6.34 seconds; we had a lot of work to do. My experience with cancer and amputation taught me to look for positives in the negatives. Riding an ill-handling bike taught me how to handle it when the engine wasn't perfect, and despite the mediocre performances we weren't hurting parts mechanically.

We entered our our first competition event, the Nitro Slam. This wasn't a quiet local round, but a two-day event in the ANDRA Top Fuel Motorcycle championship, televised nationally, with thirteen professional teams entered. The first day was qualifying and the second day was eliminations – a tournament of the quickest eight riders. We didn't do well on our first qualifying run but as night fell I had a second attempt to qualify for race day. The lights of Perth Motorplex blazed on to the drag strip and many spectators watched from the sidelines, glued to the sight of the fierce nitro bikes. This time when I opened the throttle, everything was different; I was launching hard and the acceleration didn't fall away. I could see my opponent out just in front of me and I was keeping pace, then I was passing him! I was aware of my front wheel sailing in the air, just like it should. As I neared the finish line I heard the tone of my engine change as one my cylinders stopped firing, but I was still carrying enough speed to cross for a 7.43 second time, which put us into the number six qualifying position with one session of qualifying remaining. The team were ecstatic with the performance, as we'd just improved our personal best time by over half a second. We didn't improve in the final qualifying session, but neither did anyone behind us in the order, so we locked in our place for the race day tournament – an amazing accomplishment at our first event.

I looked at the run sheets after qualifying was complete and saw I would be up against a former Australian champion in the first round. I was expecting a tough introduction to racing, but I had a stroke of luck when he announced his bike was broken and he was not able to front for the race. I didn't like winning by default and I would rather have earned my first round win, but the bye run was important to the team, because it gave us a free pass to keep building our experience. I lined up alone for the first round and launched the bike, my eyes wide as the horsepower was unleashed. But then something felt wrong, like everything on the bike was loose; the whole chassis started to shake and I had to get off the throttle. The bike slowed down and I began to analyse the problem in my head, noticing how detached the steering felt. We returned the bike to the pits and my team discovered all of the steering had shaken loose, with the front end of the bike just sitting in place, almost ready to fall out. We hadn't thought to check over the steering and forks of the bike in our pre-race checks and it became a learning experience for us all about how violent the vibrations could be with a nitro motor.

We tightened every nut and bolt we could find on the bike, and added shims to the front end to give it more tension on the bearings. We were in the semi finals, where we would take on the current Australian champion Chris Matheson. We were David against Goliath but I had nothing for Chris's power and I kept pace for all of about 60 feet before he was tearing off into the distance. Meanwhile, my bike started heading for Chris's lane and I had to abandon the run. I just didn't have the experience yet to catch my bike in time to correct it.

I don't like any loss, but the sting didn't last long as I reflected on what we had achieved at our first race event. We were a green team who were still learning how to start this nitro bike without it exploding, but I was a semi finalist and only the reigning champion was there to stop me.

At a moment of success, as the adrenaline flowed, much of my struggle was forgotten. Barely six months earlier I couldn't walk, and while I was always confident I would walk again (and much more), I never knew for sure until I'd actually achieved the goals. I found that one way to achieve goals was to set a much bigger one for the future. Instead of just concentrating on walking unassisted, I told myself I wanted to set the walking record, because if I broke the record that meant achieving all the small goals along the way. The Nitro Harley worked the same way and I set my sights on becoming the world's quickest amputee on two wheels, which meant breaking the 7.07 second record held by the USA's Reggie Showers.

The nitro gods were fickle. After my initial success in reaching the semi final at my first event, I struggled for the rest of my first season. I desperately wanted to beat Reggie's record and run a 'six', a 6.99 second time or better, before the season was finished but I just couldn't make it happen. I didn't have a big budget to pay someone to set up my bike, so the only way to develop the tune up was to take the time to learn and experiment ourselves as a team. We were still on the learning curve and doing things the hard way but that is not to say we didn't have people helping us along the way. The bike's original builder, Brett Stevens, flew to Perth for a couple of events to give us a hand and Uncle Phil decided he wanted to come and join the party too. Phil had travelled all over the country with Uncle Kim and learned plenty about nitro in that time; I un-

Nitro on dirt – chasing a rush!

derestimated how much he knew. In retrospect I should have approached him much earlier about joining the team.

Once the summer drag racing season finished in Western Australia, there was a small dirt drag racing series that began. There were three major events near the towns of Bindoon, Turner Gully and Westdale, where Nitro Harleys rode over an eighth mile (201 metre) sand track. I'd seen these crazy guys before and the thought occurred to me that it might not be too hard to put the bike on to dirt and get back to my off road roots. A lot of the riders used older chassis that had seen the end of their useful life on regular drag strips, but I saw no reason why we couldn't make some adaptations to my bike and have a play. We had to use a paddle tyre on the rear, which worked by scooping up dirt and throwing it behind the bike to get traction, and a motocross-style tyre on the front.

We tuned the bike to cater for the reduced load on the motor and I had a blast trying to put the power down to the sand. I was surprised at how much a Nitro Harley felt like riding a big dirt bike as it crabwalked the track; the biggest difference was we were clocking around 210kph through the finish line! Riding on dirt would not teach most teams a lot, but for us as a new team it meant more experience and that was something we could not get enough of.

I thought my second season might be easier, but we were getting a tough introduction to nitro. We went through a whole season and did not make any progress whatsoever. We were putting in a lot of hard work without many rewarding numbers, but I applied the same mindset that got me through cancer and the amputation. I had picked my goals and only I could make them happen. We were still getting to play with bikes, we weren't damaging too much gear mechanically and we weren't getting hurt ourselves. With a second season behind me I thought about how we could move forward for the third.

During the winter break, I delved more into understanding how my motorcycle worked. I obtained a cheat sheet, which described how the chassis was built and where I could make adjustments to change the handling. It was like finding the Rosetta Stone, and all of the complicated elements on the motorcycle that didn't make sense apart came together to form a language, expressed in how the bike moved under power. I made a lot of adjustments across the chassis, like altering the rear tyre offset and changing the way I positioned myself on the bike. There were lots of 'one percenters' adding up and I couldn't wait for spring to come so I could go drag racing again.

Perth Motorplex re-opened after winter with a test day, and I had a feeling we might be in for something big with the bike, but I wondered if I was going to be able to handle this beast at its full potential. We waited in the staging lanes for our turn to run, high on expectations. As we were called forward and the bike was fired up underneath me it felt good, and then everything just clicked. The bike left the start line hard and true, with a new level of aggression. I didn't have to correct my steering much as I punched second gear right on cue, the soft rear tyre growing in size from the centrifugal force and lifting the front wheel higher and higher off the ground. The bike veered a little to the left in the second half of the track and it was all I could do to keep the throttle pinned until the finish line as the speed built. The end of the quarter mile passed in a blurred flash and I shifted my body into the airflow and released the parachute to slow the old girl down. Some people say the quickest runs feel slow, but this run felt genuinely fast and as I pulled the bike to a stop I pumped my fist in the air, sure that I had run a good number. I waited at the end of the track for my pit crew to come and pick me up, heart pumping, and as they approached they started screaming and cheering. "6.96!" I'd made my first six second run and I was the quickest amputee on two wheels anywhere in the world! The rush of success flooded through me as the numbers sank in.

Being able to run that first six second pass was among one of the best days of my life. It was something I set out to achieve and when it happened it was a surreal moment. I thought back to laying in the hospital telling Clint about what I was going to do next. Reaching this goal was a massive weight off my shoulders, yet I wanted to set a new goal right away and get straight to the next thing. Going to race in America sounded good to me.

Running the six was a long time coming and it was a sweet victory to have. I liked that it was well executed; we had a plan and it worked. And through those first tough seasons I had learned how to ride a bike that was being difficult, which would make full power runs much easier. Drag racing is like many other things in life, where when you achieve something once it becomes easier and easier. I've since run many more six second passes but that first one will remain the most special. Motorsport had always given me a high, but this was the first time I'd done something people around the world would notice and I felt strong pride in the achievement.

With the record now set, I also wanted an event win – numbers were fine but drag racing was all about beating the man or woman in the lane next to me. I entered an event called the Goldenstates. Like the Nitro Slam, this was a nationally televised championship event for Top Fuel Motorcycles, but it was unique because it featured two individual rounds over two nights, each with a different winner, giving us two chances to get our shit together. On the first day we didn't have much luck and we lost early, but our fortunes changed on the second day.

The race format was a shortened version where teams qualified in the first round, then raced for a spot in the finals in the second round. We qualified third with a 6.98 time, some way off the leader's 6.52 but enough to be competitive. In the first round we secured the win with a 6.97 second time, consistent but still not world-beating. Good news arrived however, as I was told my time was quick enough to be seeded in the final round! The bad news was that we were up against one of Australia's quickest Nitro Harleys.

There's a saying in drag racing that consistency is what will win races, and we had that on our side. I returned to my thoughts of focusing on the positive instead of the negatives, just like I had done when we started learning on the bike. I decided to make a tactical call for the final round. We didn't have the outright horsepower to win the final, even if we stepped up the tune radically, but on this night we had a motorcycle that was predictable and repeating, and that meant something. I decided to leave the tune up alone and stay in our consistency window. Once the clutch and fuel system were set in the pits, I had no way to change them before the race and as my bike was towed from the pits to the staging lanes, I wondered if I had made the right decision. It went against my nature not to try and improve my performances on every run and the weather was cooling rapidly, adding to the risk that our tune up would move out of the comfortable zone we had found.

My eyes gazed toward the start line area where officials were motioning us forward; it was our turn in the spotlight. This was where the value of my team and their experience culminated, I had to trust that they had done their job and now it was time to do mine. We were functioning as a unit, with precision and calmness, as the electric starter was attached to my bike. The starter whirred over and the engine fired lazily into life on methanol, before the nitro fuel began to flow with its staccato symphony. I rolled forward for the final clash of the event. Up until this point the engines had just been idling but as we moved into our burnouts we hit the throttle and smoked in the start line. My crew performed their last duties and moved back, and my brother Luke gave me a slap on the back as I inched closer to the start line. I readied myself as the staging lights glowed in the night; ready for the green light, I knew this was my shot.

The extra adrenaline helped my reaction time and I had an early jump. Despite how much attention I was giving my own run, my ears pricked as I heard my opponent's bike rev high opposite me, normally a sign that it has overpowered the track and spun the tyre. More adrenaline coursed through my veins as my mind analysed the race, it sounded like there were problems in the other lane and I had to keep the throttle pinned no matter what. My own engine tone was off – the clutch was slipping, a consequence of our safe tune up not suiting the cooling night temperatures, but I didn't give up. The bike made a move for the safety barriers and I shifted my body weight to correct it as I hustled for the finish line, passing 200kph, then 300kph. I thundered over the finish line stripe and my heart raced with the realisation – victory!

My crew came to pick me from the end of the track in record time, cheering and slapping me on the back. They informed me I had not only won the race but I'd broken the much sought after 200mph barrier for the first time, with a top speed of 202mph (326kph). I told my brother Luke before the race to make sure he brought a pocket knife with him in case I won, because my leathers and racing boots were taped together around my prosthetic leg to ensure it stayed attached on a run. I rushed to cut the tape away so I could celebrate in a unique way when I received my trophy.

I was interviewed for the TV coverage and then waited for my name to be called up during trophy presentations. I made a speech and sprayed some champagne around before I sat down on the edge of the podium to remove my prosthetic leg. I poured in the champagne and drank straight from the sweaty carbon fibre bowl. I saw plenty of wide eyes around me but the reactions quickly transformed from shock to celebration.

In the days after winning, I decided I needed to take action on my next goal – to race in the USA. Amputation didn't slow me down, if anything I decided I was going to attack life harder. People in my life tried to warn me and told me it was time to settle down, that the cancer and amputation were warning signs. They meant well, but they didn't realise a life at slow speed would not make me happy. Everyone has a different mission in life and I wanted to live mine to the fullest. Any one of us can be diagnosed with a terminal illness, or have an event that changes our lives. Are you going to be happy and say you lived your life to the fullest if that happens?

There has been other amputee drag racers before, but I don't think anyone has ever done a 'leggy'! Typical of me I guess, turning everything into a reason for a drink.

My Brother's Keeper

Racing a Nitro Harley required a strong team around me and I was proud to watch my brother Luke become the foundation of the pit crew. Giving somebody responsibility is a great way to see what they are made of, and as I gave Luke more important roles on the bike I was seeing the strongest elements of his personality revealed; his growing confidence in his abilities was a pleasure to watch. He learned a lot in a short time – not many other 20 year olds could say they were crew chief on a Nitro Harley, but Luke could. As I concentrated on the clutch and fuel systems, I could leave everything else to Luke. He managed the other members of the team and I learned to trust his judgement.

When I first bought the Nitro Harley, Luke was still a teenager, but a couple of years made all the difference in his attitude. He was a mechanic by trade, and he thought he knew it all, but nitro demanded attention in areas a regular motor did not. He was involved with our first season on he bike, but he needed some time just standing back to be able to understand the responsibility involved with maintaining a nitro engine. But once we had some experience, I waited for Luke to give me a pat on the back to tell me that everything was set on the start line. If he didn't pat me I wondered what the little shit had done wrong, because he was probably worried!

Luke has always been my right hand man as a little brother and a friend. Mum and Dad said he was a surprise, and coming along almost a full decade after I did, I believe them. Surprise or not, Luke was the golden child growing up and could do no wrong. I do believe we were raised differently, and it seemed like I used to cop a hiding for the things Luke could get away with. We both took traits from our father, and Luke's was that he always thought he was right. No matter how many times I told him he was wrong he wouldn't listen and we could argue about the colour of a blue sky. He might've been stubborn, but we grew up as close brothers.

I've always looked out for my little brother and he has been a loyal partner in crime, especially for my pranks. I remember one time in particular where Luke helped me pull off one of the funniest pranks of my life. One of my mates thought it would be a great joke to get my tools out of my ute and put them under the tyres. He tied the tape measure around the tailshaft for good measure. I was a regular shit stirrer, but he thought he finally had one up on me. When I saw what he had done, I came up with a plan for revenge. Luke and Dad had been out crabbing several days previous and I asked if they still had the shells buried somewhere.

"Lukey, I want you to put on some gloves, overalls and a mask and dig those crabs out and put them in a box," I said. I'm not sure he even asked why, he just did it. It took me about half an hour to drive to the house while poor Luke dug out foul smelling, maggot-filled blue manna crab husks. He vomited into his mask as he picked up the rotting carcasses by hand and filled a box. He took them to my ute and sealed up the box, putting a spare tyre on top to keep the smell inside. All I could say was, "I owe you for this."

I drove to my mate's house where I spread the whole box of fermenting crustaceans across his front lawn and garden. Later that evening he arrived home to an awful smell, and he didn't realise where it was coming from until he saw all the neighbourhood cats on his front lawn enjoying a seafood dinner. He spat the dummy at me, really went off the dial actually, but that's what he gets for playing a prank on me! Luke was the little legend who made it happen.

Bikes have always been our major shared interest. When we were young I built small jumps for him to learn on, and Luke always had whatever bike he wanted – he just had to ask Dad. One year he was given a Honda CRF250 for Christmas, a proper quick race bike. It was the first powerful two wheeler Luke had and I told Dad Luke was going to hurt himself on it. Surely enough, by lunchtime on Christmas Day, the bike had thrown him off and Luke was in hospital for a broken wrist.

Perhaps that was a sign, because Luke hasn't had too much luck with cars and bikes over the years. He left school in Year 11 and begun a mechanic's apprenticeship with our family friend Travis at Ningaloo Automotive Repairs in Exmouth. This was when the nursery was wrapping up and Dad wanted to get out of Perth for a while, so the timing worked out well. I think Luke has had five cars to date and all of them have ended up broken or wrecked, because he loves to fuck with the motors until they are beyond recognition.

After starting with a Nissan Patrol, Luke's first fast car was a Holden Commodore VT with a V8, which he bought a couple of days before our Nanna's funeral. Nanna loved burnouts, and though she pretended to be mad she enjoyed watching us get up to mischief. After her funeral, we had a wake at the Left

Bank pub and then went to Uncle Phil's. Many family members were there and we carried on into the night, and I thought it would be great to do a big burnout in tribute to Nanna, using Luke's Commodore. It was a fantastic burnout, but Luke got upset with me afterwards about thrashing his car. Uncle Phil chimed in, "You gave your brother the keys, what did you expect?"

Luke did a big burnout of his own not long after, unfortunately right in front of a police car, and he was booked under Western Australia's tough anti-hoon laws and the car was impounded. Unfortunately that wouldn't be his only run-in with the law. At the time he was living with me and he owned a little XR50 mini bike that he could ride to his friend Travis' house, who then took him to work. He would ride down the footpath, through the bush and pop out near Travis' place, but Luke must have been reported by someone, because one day the cops were waiting for him. He saw them up ahead and was able to disappear before they noticed him. After a close call like that, what did Luke do? He went the exact same way the next day and again the cops were waiting for him, but this time they picked him up. The bike was added to the list of confiscations and his licence suspension was extended.

The next car he bought was a Mercedes, with airbagged suspension, a turbo Nissan RB20 motor and all done up, but by the time he sold the car it was not running. Luke loves a project, he just doesn't like finishing them. He actually got good money for the Merc and I urged him to buy a reliable Toyota Hilux ute, a car he could use for work and own outright. He went searching and then showed me some pics of a terrible blue Hilux worth a couple of grand, and I pleaded with him not to buy it. But Luke was stubborn and this was the Hilux he wanted, so he bought it and within a week it had dramas and ended up on jack stands. He sold the rims to get a new motor, but then of course he had no rims, so he sold it as it was – no wheels or anything. He later bought a nicer Hilux and that was the first car I think he took pride in. He put on a roof rack, an awning and spot lights and it was perfect for him.

As far as two wheels go, Luke is as fast as me on flat land but freestyle proved difficult for him. I think you need a part of your brain missing to be good at freestyle, the part that calculates risk! Luke must have had one ball too many and his confidence was cracked by a few spills he had early while he was still learning to jump. I could tell him how fast to hit a jump and he did everything right and committed, but then fear froze his body. He had a bad moment when his feet got caught when he tried a trick, and another time he landed flat on his stomach. Those incidents made him give freestyle a miss from then on – a sensible decision. But still, he could get on any bike and ride the wheels off it.

Once Luke finished his mechanic's apprenticeship he wanted to try different occupations and in 2016 he started working full time for my landscaping business. Luke pretty much ran the labour side of things for me. I could leave him with a job, tell him what I needed, and he always delivered what I had asked for and more; his skill and work ethic were second to none. I trusted him with big jobs while I could go out and procure more work. We sometimes had disagreements about the right way to do particular jobs, but we generally got to the same result even if we took different paths. I had to learn to trust his judgement, and he was often correct. We had a tight brotherly bond, which was made even stronger when Luke decided to live with me as well.

After seeing Luke's commitment to my race team, I started looking for a second bike to put him on because I was confident he would be a brilliant drag racer. I let him do a burnout on mine and he smoked it up better than I did the first time; he was a natural. We were in the midst of planning a trip to America, where there was a bike for sale that I was keen on for Luke. We were going to crew on the bike together and see what it was like, and I had even organised a ride for a national event.

On May 4, 2017 we had a big day. Luke was working with me with an early morning start picking up skip bins – a side hustle we were running at the time. We found strong demand for the business but it took a lot of time and effort to move the bins around, and so we planned to put the bins on hold because it was getting too hard for both of us to operate alongside landscaping.

Once Luke had finished with the skip bins he came back to the yard to help work on a race trailer I was selling. We had a buyer coming to see the trailer and only some finishing touches remained, when one of the young fellas working for me drilled straight through a hydraulic ram that was critical to move the tailgate up and down. I was running around like a madman trying to get a replacement before our potential buyer arrived.

We found a new cylinder and Luke, being a master mechanic, started installing it. Replacing the ram was a tricky, messy, headfuck of a job and by the end of it Luke was covered in grease from head to toe. However the standard was 110%, like everything he did, and I was confident in his work. We knocked off at 4.30pm, and Luke was headed for the shops to get a new phone, and then he was going to pick up some burnout tyres for another car he was mucking around with. I told him I would catch up with him later, and he drove out.

I returned home from work and was shortly headed back out the door, going to meet some friends. As I sat down to tie my shoe laces, my phone began ringing with a private number. Normally I wouldn't answer, but for some reason I swiped the call. It was the police, and they said my brother had been in a car accident.

I got in my car and raced to Nicholson Road, where I arrived at a three-car accident scene that looked like a scrap yard, with twisted metal and shrapnel glinting across the road in the setting sun. The police had the road blocked off at both ends, but from a distance I could discern Luke's car and see it was totalled. I walked through the road block but a police officer told me I couldn't go any further, even when I explained I'd just received a call telling me to get to the scene. Perhaps it was a lack of communication, but when the officer turned his back to get on the radio I walked straight past to get to my brother.

"Fuck, here we go," I thought as I approached Luke's car. One side looked intact, but as I walked closer the other side of the car revealed the impact, severely damaged from the front bumper to the end of the rear cargo tray. It did not look survivable and I had no idea what I was going to see when I saw Luke, not knowing how injured he was or if he was alive. I took rapid breaths as I moved closer.

Never in my life had I seen someone I cared about in such a mess, normally it was me laying there all busted up. The moment gave me a surreal vision, as I understood how everyone around me felt during my accidents, or seeing me undergoing chemotherapy. All of these people cared about me, and it dawned on me how they felt when they couldn't do anything about my pain. I had confidence in myself and I would always be telling people I was fine, I'd survive, but this was a reality check on the emotions they had to deal with; they weren't sure what the outcome was going to be. I wanted to put myself in Luke's position because I knew how to get through trauma, but he had never been hurt like this before. But he was alive, and that was the first step. "How are you going, cock?" I said, trying to make my brother smile.

Luke was trapped inside the car, metal bent around him. "Sorry, I'm sorry Benny, sorry," he said. I told him to be quiet, keep his chin up and we would work on getting him out. An ambulance officer was inside the car with Luke, administering painkillers and keeping him calm and happy, or at least as happy as he could be in a wrecked Toyota Hilux. The other paramedic seemed to have no interest in getting Luke out, which I thought was strange at the time.

Luke was stable and the paramedic said it was time for the firefighters to work on cutting him out. I helped rip the back seat out and then I climbed inside the car to support the roof with my back as they begun to cut out the side pillars with the Jaws of Life. The firefighters were cautious when cutting the car open, because relieving pressure in one area of the wreck had the potential to apply pressure in other places. Luke's broken body was caught between the metal, his arm tangled up and broken in the frame of the door, which had been torn open during the accident. I held Luke as the giant, pneumatic can openers did their job. It seemed to take an age to cut enough of the car apart to get Luke out, but eventually we had space to move him on to a stretcher. The last step was lifting the collapsed steering wheel and column, which had broken Luke's femur.

Once Luke was freed, I extracted myself from the mess of metal and watched as he was attended to by the paramedics on the stretcher. He kept telling me he was sorry he was going to be off work, and I joked back with him to keep him smiling and happy. Things were so serious that there were thoughts of calling in the rescue helicopter, but the ambulance was going to be well on its way to Royal Perth Hospital before the helicopter could arrive.

For once I had a ride in the front seat of the ambulance. The paramedic who I had seen standing back at the scene now stepped up, driving like a man possessed, and I understood his role. We were flying at high speed along the freeway and despite the serious circumstances I was enjoying the ride; the driver was breaking all the road rules except he was on the right side of the law. He drove the ambulance flat out past speed cameras, which flashed in vain as he casually waved for a laugh. He even ran a car off the side of the road, a little Hyundai Excel that swerved straight into deep sand as he cracked up laughing. "What a maniac, I should have been an ambulance driver," I thought.

Luke was still saying he was sorry from the back of the ambulance. "Benny, I've spoiled the trip to America. We can't go anymore." We were weeks away from our trip to the USA.

"Don't worry about America," I said. "Because if you can't go that ain't going to stop me!" Lukey sighed and the paramedics in the ambulance laughed. I was revving him up, trying to take his thoughts away from the pain. America was the last thing on my mind.

We arrived at Royal Perth Hospital, which is not the nicest of places to be even on a sunny day. Luke was admitted into emergency, stabilised by the doctors and it seemed like it was all going to be happy days. My girlfriend Jess arrived and together with Luke we went through the admission paperwork. Luke had never been admitted to a public hospital before, because he was under Mum and Dad's private health insurance, so we had some paperwork to do. I wrote down his details and as we got to the section for next-of-kin, he said he wanted to list me as the one making decisions on his behalf and receiving the information on his condition. Luke didn't want the pressure of Mum and Dad knowing every detail about his hospital stay, as he had seen the strange reactions from the family when I had cancer. I knew Luke needed a positive environment and I thought by serving as his next-of-kin I could help deliver that.

Despite the severity of the wreck, Luke was stable and it seemed as though the Stevens lads had survived yet another close call. He was drinking orange juice and eating yoghurt, and I felt confident enough to leave him in hospital for the night. Jess and I left for home to get some sleep and Luke called my phone around midnight, telling me he was getting operated on the next day. He was clear minded enough to remember my phone number, as he didn't have his mobile phone with him, and I told him I would be in to see him after his operation.

I knew Luke was going in for his operation the next day and I waited a few hours before I tried calling the phone next to his bed to see how it went. I couldn't get through to Luke so I called the hospital through the day, searching for updates. They told me everything was fine and that it was a low risk operation with little chance of complications. I felt like I was getting fobbed off, and soon most of the day had passed without any additional information. I got fed up and drove to the hospital, where I visited the familiar trauma ward and looked for Luke.

"We believe Luke is out of his operation and has been taken to the intensive care unit because he hasn't woken up," the staff told me. "It could have been a bigger dose of anaesthesia and they will just have him there until he wakes up."

It sounded odd, like nobody quite knew what was happening. I took the long walk to intensive care, where I waited for more information. The delay seemed strange, like they didn't know what was happening or where Luke was. There was an intercom on the door I had buzzed when I arrived, so I tried buzzing it again to see if somebody would come out. Finally a man arrived to give me information, but he seemed scared to tell me what was going on. He couldn't speak English very well and was talking in circles about where my brother was.

"Cut the bullshit, what the fuck is wrong with my fucking brother?" I said.

The swearing caught him by surprise and made him talk more clearly. "Your brother has not woken up from the operation," he said.

"Will he wake up?" I asked.

"I don't know."

"Will he survive?"

"I don't know."

I still had no real idea what was going on, or direction on where to next. I understood that a patient's condition was not always certain, but I wanted information. This guy was as useless as tits on a bull and here he was working in intensive care and looking after my brother! I was annoyed after the non-conversation, but the man allowed me to see Luke. He looked completely different to how I had left him the night before; now he was covered in tubes, with all sorts of equipment hanging off him and a full time nurse at his watch. I was stunned because everything had seemed normal the night before, and he had sounded fine when I spoke to him on the phone.

A new doctor came in, Dr Andy Robertson. He was the head honcho in intensive care and I asked him a single time what was going on, and he was able to tell me. He explained everything, not sparing me from the detail. Luke had a long bone fracture in his femur, which allowed bone marrow and fat to leak into his bloodstream and reach his brain, creating an embolism (a blockage of a blood vessel). The embolism had been discovered during a routine CT scan after his morning operation and Luke was now in a coma. Fat embolisms are extremely rare; there were very few symptoms and not much can be done to cure them. According to the hospital staff, Luke had felt very tired before the operation and seemed like he was away with the fairies, but none of that was unusual for someone who had been in a major accident. With hindsight, the embolism was likely already forming and when Luke laid down for the operation it exacerbated the problem. At that stage no one had any idea the embolism was lurking.

I stayed with Luke all day and all night in the hospital, not knowing when – or if – my brother would wake up. I slept literally across the corridor from where I woke up to a stump on my right leg three years previous, give or take a day. I would need that experience now to guide my brother through his greatest challenge.

Realising Recovery

On the night Luke had the accident, I had called Mum and Dad to tell them, letting them know everything was under control. He only needed a simple operation on some broken bones after all, and it wasn't like he had a head injury or anything – not at the time. Mum wanted Luke to call her after the operation, and when he didn't get in touch she started calling me. I explained how he hadn't woken up from the operation, probably because he was very tired, but he would be okay. That was a white lie, but I didn't want Mum and Dad rushing into the hospital yet, because that was going to make life harder for the doctors and Luke.

My family is different to most, with lots of powerful personalities that react differently to stressful situations. Dad was unpredictable, Mum was overbearing and both were prone to misunderstanding information, which could have bad consequences for Luke. The decisions I was making at the time were hard enough, knowing that the reality could be devastating for my brother. Most families handle a crisis better together, but we were not most families.

I made the decision to withhold telling them about the embolism until I had a proper understanding myself. Mum began ringing the hospital and even though she was not listed as next of kin, a staff member told her Luke was in intensive care. Shortly she was back on the phone to me, demanding to know why Luke was in intensive care when I had said he was okay. She persisted and then announced she was going to come to the hospital. It sounds harsh, but I wanted to do everything I could to keep Mum and Dad away until I understood everything myself so the best decisions could be made for Luke. I worried Mum would be on Facebook telling the world what had happened, before we even had clarity ourselves, making Luke's friends and family worry unnecessarily. I spoke to her and said she should come the following day when we knew more information, and she agreed.

My recovery from cancer, dozens of hospital trips and an amputation had given me valuable experience in rehabilitation and I understood what it took to get through mentally. Luke needed positive, constructive and happy people around him. Though he was not responsive, I was sure that he could still sense what was happening around him. I believed he would pick up on stress and worry. I organised with Mum to come and see Luke, but I didn't want Dad there yet. I had no idea what state of mind he was in, and Luke would be affected by negative reactions.

When Mum arrived, I gave her a briefing before she went into the hospital room, telling her not to cry because even though Luke was in a coma he still knew what was going on around him. I hadn't told her about the embolism yet, just that he was in an induced coma to rest his body, and I asked her to speak positively and normally, to let Luke know she was there and ready to support him. This was how she could best help him through this tough time.

Mum was the first person besides me to see Luke in a coma, and it was difficult to watch. He was laying there lifeless with all this medical equipment hanging off him, just like a movie. To her credit, Mum was tough and sat by his side and spoke softly and kindly to him, like a mother should. She couldn't do much to help him yet but she had her emotions in check and I couldn't ask for more at that stage - the calm love was exactly what Luke needed. The visit went well and everything seemed under control.

The only other people who knew about Luke's condition were Uncle Kim, Uncle Phil and Terry Dorrington, the Perth Motorplex chaplain. They provided me with a compass for my actions, especially in regards to the family; they knew what we were like and were able to see the scenario objectively. I was well aware this was not a normal situation, keeping my immediate family at arm's length, but the priority was Luke and everything I was doing was based on my own experience. The best guidance for him was going to be via my trauma and I knew it was important to keep his environment as positive as possible. Kim, Phil, and especially Terry were there to take me aside if I was wrong, but their thoughts echoed my own. Each day I left home at 5.30am to get to Royal Perth Hospital by 7am, and I stayed until 8pm every night, waiting for some small movement or sign of hope with Luke. I stalked Dr Robertson on his rounds, trying to learn as much as I could about fat embolisms. I discovered the recovery rate was normally good, but there was a chance that if the embolism was widespread then Luke may never wake up again. If he didn't wake up, it was going to be our choice to keep him alive or not. If he did wake up, there was also a high chance he was going to be confined to a wheelchair.

Luke was given an MRI scan and the results weren't positive.

The doctors confirmed the fat embolism, and it was widespread. If it had been a blood clot, like a stroke, Luke would have been done for, but a major difference between a fat embolism and a stroke is that fat dissolves, unlike a blood clot. That meant if Luke could get through the worst part, this first stage, he had a fighting chance at recovery. Armed with this information, I began to consider Luke's rehabilitation and what the best path might be. The lessons I had learned from my bad times would be vital to Luke now if he was to lead a normal life again.

Luke had to meet a set of criteria to show improvement, but not many positive signs were seen in the first week. He could breathe by himself but he still needed assistance from the machine; his body alone could not be trusted. He had a tube down his throat which irritated him, getting a vague sensory response as he chewed on it or coughed a little. But otherwise he was just laid out having a good old sleep with no movement or responses. There was fuck-all I could do apart from being there with him, and the doctor visited each day to say there were no signs of improvement.

"Well that's obvious, he's not exactly sitting up with us eating cake, is he?" I'd think to myself. In my experience, I had found these plateaus of recovery were the most difficult time to stay optimistic as the patient, let alone as a relative watching on, but my role here was to stay confident and positive for my brother.

My family's concerns were growing about Luke. I'd given my sister Jodi the same information as I had given Mum and Dad, but until Luke's condition developed further there was nothing more to say; he was stable and alive, but I had no idea when we would see improvement. My sister and I got along okay and we used to look out for each other as kids, but in recent years our relationship had been at a distance. She lived in Tasmania and

I explained Luke's situation to her over the phone the same as I had to Mum, but afterwards Mum spoke to her and confused much of the information. I had said the same thing to Jodi, Mum and Dad but they all came away with different thoughts on what was wrong with Luke. These cross-wired messages were what I was first concerned about.

Jodi called me and was angry, saying she wanted to be updated in person rather than seeing it on Facebook. Apart from a simple status update saying Luke had been in an accident, I hadn't posted anything on social media. Jodi told me she deserved to know about Luke's condition and I repeated to her what I had told Mum and Dad. I kept it deliberately simple, for Luke's sake, and said I would let her know if she needed to make a quick plane trip over. Unfortunately, Mum was putting posts up on Facebook and confusing Jodi, and Jodi thought if she flew over she would not be allowed to see Luke because Mum had said I was controlling access. I had been listed as next-of-kin but I certainly wasn't stopping Mum visiting.

"Mum keeps calling me crying because you won't let her in the room, so what chance will I have?" she said.

The stories were getting mixed and I felt like I was a target, even as I was trying to do the best for Luke. Jodi said she and Luke had always been close, and she did not like being kept in the dark on the opposite side of Australia. She wanted to be there when he was awake to talk to him, so I said that she had nothing stopping her flying to Perth, and not to point fingers if she didn't want to fly over. She called me a miserable asshole for telling her she couldn't see her brother – something I had never done. We both had love for our brother but we expressed it in different ways. Her love came through emotion and concern, mine with a determined focus on making a path for Luke's recovery, a result of my experiences.

I was dealing with the family and at the same time trying to figure out what we were going to do about Luke. I was under the pump, and I began to wonder if I was doing the right thing. If everyone around me smelt like an asshole, there was a good chance it might have been me. I was stressed about the family and called Uncle Kim to seek his advice, because he knew the family better than anyone.

"Benny, do not change a thing," he said. "The only way Luke is getting through this is with you. You need to keep going with what you are doing."

Kim's confidence gave me a boost just when I needed it. Jodi did decide to make the flight over and like I did with Mum, I laid out the ground rules: only positive conversation and love for Luke, no family fighting or smart-ass remarks, and we would meet in reception at 9am to take her to the room.

Jodi arrived early and called to ask if she could go into Luke's room. I told her I would be there soon and she would have to wait; I was worried she would walk in alone and break down at the sight of Luke. If Luke was in a coma and couldn't see his condition, but could hear everyone entering the room immediately start crying, what was he going to think? When I got to the hospital, I asked Jodi to walk out of Luke's room if she needed to cry and come back when she was done. We walked in and she broke down in tears as soon as she saw him. She went outside, took a break and once she got through her emotions, she sat beside Luke and stayed strong for him, showing their brother-sister bond, and I hoped she could be another positive force for his recovery.

I thought we were on our way to avoiding any drama in the family, but Mum was logged into Dad's Facebook account on her phone and I could see messages going back and forth between Jodi and Dad. They called me 'Lord Ben' for how I was managing Luke's visits and decisions on his behalf, and I worried they were going to undermine all the progress we were making with Luke. They saw me as selfish and controlling, but I knew my brother needed the best environment possible and I was willing to do whatever it took to give him that.

The hospital wanted to hurry along Luke's progress after a slow first week. They replaced some of the tubes going into Luke's mouth with a tracheotomy. Apparently in the past, a tracheotomy had helped the small amount of people who had experienced a fat embolism. It seemed to make a difference and Luke looked more comfortable with the tracheotomy in place. The hospital took him off 'red alert' status and shifted him back to the trauma ward.

The changes were slow, but Luke began checking off progress boxes, and each one made my heart grow for his future. His eyes opened and he begun to search the room when he heard voices, though he still wasn't able to track objects. After a few more days he started tracking, following people as they entered the room. Then the smiles returned, as he started grinning from one side of his face. A wave of pure relief came as Luke was finally able to show emotion. His brain was following the developmental steps of an infant, learning everything from scratch. It was like he was growing up again in fast forward.

I researched ways to help Luke's progress, and found out that bringing familiar people to visit could help activate different areas in his brain. I invited Uncle Kim and Uncle Phil, Nitro Harley drag racer Ian Ashelford, our friend Point, and Perth Motorplex volunteer Carole Borkowski, all people who Luke had memories with. Every couple of days I brought someone new from the extended family to come and speak with Luke. I focused on finding people he thought were funny, because his laughter was one of the most positive signs that he could listen and interpret what was happening around him.

Uncle Russy was one of the best jokers in our group and I asked him to visit Luke and do whatever he could to make my brother laugh. Russy is the crudest person at the best of times and Luke smiled as soon as Russy came in, his eyes lighting up with anticipation. Russy told Luke how one day he climbed up a tree and asked Uncle Kim to trick my step grandfather Mike into standing underneath. With target in place, Russy dropped his pants and took a dump from the tree branch with precision normally reserved for US air strikes. You wouldn't believe someone could be so accurate with their ass. Luke burst out into laughter, true vocal laughter, not just wheezing. We were bringing back his memories and his mind step by step.

Mum was there every day in support of Luke, and she had learned much over the years about dealing with trauma, but her emotions sometimes got the better of her. She would lay on him and wrap her arms around his body, and I could tell it was bothering Luke because his heart rate went up; the numbers on the machine changed in front of us. I pointed this out to Mum and explained to her I wasn't being spiteful, she just needed to give him some room. When Mum sat back Luke's heart rate dropped again. Eventually she understood that just being there and being positive was enough support. I could see she was hurting, and hugging and cuddling your son is fine to do as a parent, but Luke needed minimal stress right now.

Dad didn't get too involved with Luke in the early stages. My relationship with Dad had changed much as we aged. I wasn't a boy depending on him for support, I was a man with my own life and a brother to protect. Luke chose to live with me for a reason, and I aimed to be a positive role model for him at all times.

Despite the progress Luke was making, Dad believed he was stuck with a vegetable for a son at best, and at worst he thought Luke was dying. Some of the people he worked with at the time had been in touch with me, asking if this was true, saying Dad had been talking about a funeral. The talk got back to Mum and made her even more worried. Dad was tangled up in his own world and believing what he wanted to believe. I was trying to create a positive environment and watched Luke's condition improve day after day; the negativity threatened to be contagious.

The first time Dad came to see Luke I told him about the limit on the number of visitors set in place by the hospital. Uncle Phil was dropping in quickly to say hello that morning, and I explained that once he was gone, Mum, Dad and I could spend the rest of the day with Luke. For some reason this small wait set off a hair trigger and he said Luke was fucked anyway.

I was angry at Dad's attitude, I was doing all I could to pull Luke through and he was giving up. I boiled over in the hospital.

"The best thing you can do is walk towards the lift or you're going to end up in the bed next to him," I snarled. Dad went to the waiting room and I took a few minutes to cool down in another room with Uncle Phil. I was furious with Dad, why wasn't he asking questions about how we could best help Luke or what it would take to make him better? The way he interpreted the problem was so different to how any other father would approach it. The nurses saw the heated exchange and they were understanding. They reassured me afterwards and told me that I was handling everything very well, which gave me confidence that I was still doing the right thing for my brother.

As the day went on, Dad was pissed off about being put in his place. The anger of his personality came out, as it regularly did when he was told he wasn't right. He started to send me abusive text messages, telling me I was to blame because I made Luke start work early in the morning before the accident. He tried to have me believe I was making all the wrong decisions. He thought Luke was dying, but I knew Luke would emerge as a survivor.

In the background, Mum was listening to Dad's influence. She went to see a new social worker and sought to become Luke's next-of-kin. The social worker was rude from day one and provided no help in the situation whatsoever, only making things harder for Luke and the family than what they needed to be.

The first social worker we had in the intensive care unit was spot-on, she helped us so much. She agreed 100% with what I was doing because she listened to the input of the nurses, who witnessed the strange actions of my family when they came to visit Luke. She and the nurses would often joke with me about how dysfunctional the family was; they could see it with their own eyes.

This second social worker had no idea on how to deal with a dysfunctional family. She had an opinion that parents were the only ones who should be next-of-kin, without knowing anything about the history of the family. She had no depth of experience with us, and no understanding on why a father on a mix of prescription medications who already thought his son was dying would be a bad person to make decisions.

I had seen the same mindset in Dad when I had cancer. He thought I was fucked and wasn't there to get me through the darkest time of my life. This was the same father who wanted to fight when he made mistakes he couldn't own up to, always ready to trade violence for reason. The same father who kicked me out of home when I was going through chemotherapy. Dad saw the world in terms of how it affected him, not what he could do to change it positively for someone else, and that was no mindset to take into my brother's recovery.

At this point you may be questioning my methods, but it is hard to put into words just how erratic my family was. Stability was never the family's strong point and I was desperately trying to give that to my brother. I was doing everything I could to protect and help Luke and I worried this threatened to undo all of that work. Once the ward nurses heard about Mum approaching the social worker, they started telling her more about Luke, which was the last thing I wanted because Mum often mixed up medical information once it was provided to her. I had to officially tell the hospital to stop handing over Luke's details because I was his next-of-kin.

I met with the social worker and if ever I encountered a polar opposite to my personality, it was her. Where I was about solving problems, she was about creating them – it seemed like all she wanted to do was put her power to use. There are people in this world who want problems so they have something to fix, and she was one of those people, but she forgot she was dealing with a human, my brother, recovering from one of the most traumatic experiences of his life.

I was short when I talked with her because I didn't think she was helping Luke or doing her job properly, and my honesty was a mistake. I wasn't rude or disrespectful, I was just straight to the point and she did not agree. The social worker said Mum deserved to be Luke's next-of-kin, because how she would much rather speak to Mum about Luke's affairs than me.

She started getting in Mum's head about needing more details on Luke, so Mum kept going to the nurses and it really began to turn into a problem. I wanted to bring this all to an end. "Let's go into a room and I will tell you everything," I said. And I did.

I explained everything to Mum that I knew about Luke. I saw a change in her, and she said she understood and was happy for me to continued to manage Luke's recovery. I had no interest in control, only in Luke's health.

Afterwards, Mum kept asking questions like what kind of brain aneurysm Luke had. She still didn't understand the injury after I explained the details to her and that frustrated me. It showed why I didn't want her in control of Luke's affairs, because she couldn't understand the information well enough to make the correct decisions, or ask the right questions.

Unbelievably, the social worker still wasn't happy, even as Mum withdrew her request to be next-of-kin. She elevated the dispute to a tribunal to have someone new appointed regardless, because she didn't feel I was fit to manage Luke's affairs. She told me I had to seek next-of-kin in court, because she didn't believe Luke was lucid when he made the decision on the first night in the hospital. A tribunal could take months, and she said in the mean time they were planning to remove me as next-of-kin.

The social worker sent all of Luke's information through to Dad, a man who was convinced my brother was a lost cause, and my sister, who lived on the other side of the country, to become next-of-kin. The social worker hated dealing with me and was determined to have me gone, even if that put my brother's recovery at risk.

My plans to race Nitro Harleys in the USA were still in place and Luke's progress was giving me confidence that it would be okay to leave him for a couple of weeks. His recovery had been amazing to watch and he was starting to mime words again. Almost four weeks to the day after his accident I was packing my bags for the flight to the United States.

We had a little send-off in the hospital with plenty of laughs, like Uncle Kim doing a raw comedy routine that involved getting his balls out for everyone to see. I had to feel sorry for the poor person next door to Luke's room, I have no idea what they must have been thinking.

I had a roster of people set to visit Luke over the coming weeks. He was aware that I was going away for the trip we had planned together and the last thing I did before leaving was to ask him if he minded me going to America to race. I told him to be honest and I wanted it to genuinely be his decision.

"Yes," he said.

"You fucking legend," I replied. That was the first proper word I had heard through his lips since the night of the accident and I felt so proud of him. He was fighting hard and he was in good hands with the nurses and my Mum, who were giving him the positive environment he needed.

"When you come back from America, Luke will be a different person," Uncle Kim said.

I hoped he was right.

Living the Dream

When I boarded the plane for my 30 hours of travel to the USA, I felt bittersweet. I was about to realise a dream, racing internationally, but I had left my brother behind. I wanted him on the journey too, but I felt confident enough he would be with me at a later time, at another event.

Travelling overseas by myself was all new. I'd been on a family vacation to the USA when I was younger, but independently crossing borders, navigating airport terminals and worrying about the time of my next flight was a new thrill. Maybe not the same rush as a Nitro Harley, but travel has a way of getting the adrenaline going.

Entering America there was a different smell when I got off the plane, like a convenience store mixed with jet fumes. The memories of my first family trip to the States were triggered, in the way that only a scent can. We had a great time on that trip, and I thought of my brother in his hospital bed, continuing his recovery.

After landing in Los Angeles I continued onward to North Carolina, where I met up with Terry Stewart, a Nitro Harley drag racing veteran. He introduced me to the USA in classic fashion as we blew up some fireworks (legally for a change), had some drinks and generally enjoyed the many freedoms of America. I would be racing in Bristol, Tennessee at the National Hot Rod Association Thunder Valley Nationals. The track earned the nickname Thunder Valley because of the mountain ranges that surround the venue, producing echoes from the loud and powerful vehicles that race within its shadows. As we drove into the massive complex I was in awe at the majesty of the venue. It was literally a green, lush valley with a drag strip carved right down the middle.

I met Mike Bahnmaier, who was supplying my ride for the event. He owned a couple of Harley-Davidson dealerships and was super passionate about drag racing. The whole team were great people and we kicked off a strong friendship right away. Freddy, Drew and Randy were my pit crew for the weekend, joined by Terry and of course Mike himself. Jennifer Harrison

Ready to rumble in Bristol, Tennessee.

from ANDRA was also in town and joined us for the weekend.

I called my team 'The Hillbillys' and they wanted to know all about me, taking the time to suss me out and see if I would be a good fit for their bike. Some of the top Nitro Harley riders in the sport were at this event and 15 bikes were trying to qualify for an eight bike field, so we had our work cut out for us. To some that might be intimidating, but I figured the worst case scenario here was being a part of the biggest drag racing series in the world. That's a pretty good worst case!

I don't think I felt the atmosphere of the moment until we started up the bike for the first time in the pits. I'd walked around the track and taken photos and selfies, but when the nitro began to flow through the veins of the mechanical beast in front of me, that was when my primitive instincts woke; the ones that used to be dedicated to escaping sabre tooth tigers or hunting wooly mammoths, a survival response transformed into something I do just for kicks. I heard the rumble of the bike and I knew we were there to race. This Nitro Harley sounded tough; it was a different configuration to mine and the exhaust pipe blew wet, puddling fuel. Pop, pop, pop-a-pop, pop. As I was watching the team work on the bike it brought a rare tear of emotion to my eye. I was on the other side of the world and my brother was back home, he should have been there. I wanted him to experience this, and it didn't really occur to me how long my personal journey had been to reach this point, I just wanted Lukey there. "I'll bring him back one day," I reminded myself.

The team readied for our first qualifying pass. I have only rolled out in front of a full house of spectators a couple of times in Perth, but Bristol was a sea of people and all eyes were on the track. It was a big stage, with some big actors. Top riders like

Tii Tharpe, Jay Turner and Randal Andras rolled through the staging lanes and into the fire-up area. The mountains loomed large and the officials had an air of corporate professionalism, but I had no fear in the moment. I was there because I wanted to be there and all of my decisions had brought me to this point.

I was scheduled to run in the second pairing of the session. Ahead of me, American riders Chris Smith and Armon Furr did their burnouts, rubber smoke and nitro fumes mixing into the air I breathed in. They took the green light and Chris's run ended with a bang, as his Nitro Harley coughed and burst into flames right there on the start line. Chris danced off the bike as officials with extinguishers rushed out to douse the fire. Whether you are a rookie or a professional, nitro always remains unpredictable.

Now it was my turn. The environment around me faded and I gave complete concentration to the motorcycle underneath me. I completed the burnout and waited for the team to do their final checks, before creeping into stage and waiting for the green light. I hit the throttle and I heard the motor rev highly as my tyre spun early, forcing me to abandon the run. We had a lot of power but getting it to the track was going to be difficult.

On the second qualifying session I improved to a 7.80 second time, but was still way off the pace. Tii Tharpe was the top qualifier and he clocked a 6.38! The 'bump spot', the slowest time to make it into the race day field, was still in the seven second zone, which was achievable for us.

Hopeful my final qualifying run would put me in the top eight, we returned to the staging lanes for the last session, but again the bike had some problems and our weekend was done. I never really had the bike moving well off the start line, which was essential when I only had a few seconds of acceleration.

It would have been smart for me to fly over a week or two earlier to do some testing, but my time was better spent with Luke. While it sounds obvious, I hadn't considered that this bike wasn't like my bike. Bikes are set up for a rider more than a car is set up for a driver so to go to the other side of the world and jump on a chassis that wasn't set up for me was asking a lot of the team. I think we did the best we could under difficult circumstances.

While we didn't get to take part in race day, just turning up to try and qualify earned me a lot of respect among the other racers at the Thunder Valley Nationals. Many other teams visited our pit area during the event to have a chat and I enjoyed meeting people who shared a common passion. I liked that no one told me I was crazy, because we all were, I suppose. It didn't matter to them that I had a missing leg, because I was there with the same mission – trying to go as quick as possible on a stupid fast motorcycle.

Another racer on my team during the event, Brian Jernigan, missed the field too so the team owner Mike packed up early and headed back to home base, leaving myself, Terry and Jennifer to watch some racing and do some more socialising in the pits. After the event we drove around Tennessee some more and then returned to Terry's house for a few more days, where we didn't do a great deal besides annoying his neighbours with more fireworks.

Terry joined me in a visit to Las Vegas to finish my trip. All through my adventure in the USA, Mum had been helping Luke call me on FaceTime, and Carole from the Motorplex had been live streaming my races for him. I was very drunk at 5am during a night out on the piss at the Luxor Hotel in Vegas, when I got a call with Luke on the other end.

"Hey, Benny." My little bro was talking again! We were actually able to have a proper conversation and he was starting to become the Luke I knew again; it was like the covers had been taken off his brain. I was stunned at his progress. As well as the immediate joy of hearing him speak, it was a relief that concentrating on giving him an environment full of positivity and stimulation had paid off, proof my experiences through cancer and amputation had come to help Luke. It was the icing on the cake for the trip and as soon as I heard those words out of his mouth I desperately wanted to be home so we could talk all about the trip and enjoy being brothers.

I flew back to Australia and my first priority once I landed was to see Luke. He had been moved to Fiona Stanley Hospital for rehabilitation I and found him out in the grounds, rolling around in his wheelchair getting some fresh air and sunshine. He was talking conversationally, but with a child-like personality, and he laughed at anything and everything. If I dropped a piece of food he thought it was hilarious. His brain was lighting up again and I was so glad that my brother, as I knew him, was coming back.

It was easy for me to return after a couple of weeks away and say Luke's progress had been quick, but in reality it was grinding work for him. He had to relearn every skill a normal person took for granted, but I knew from day one he would recover quickly because he was a strong minded kid – that stubborn nature helped his healing. Still, I found it difficult to watch him get frustrated with new tasks, like when it took 30 seconds to get a piece of food from the plate to his mouth. Luke was a man who was able to race bikes, fix cars, run a business, and work on the quickest motorcycles on the planet, and now he struggled to feed himself. I had to put his recovery into perspective and remember how close I had been to losing him forever. It wasn't my role to feel sorry for him, I had to keep up my end of the bargain and work for him.

Luke was starting to remember parts of his life, albeit somewhat scattered. While I was in America, I bought some pink racing leathers to fundraise for him, with the idea that I would wear them if we reached a target. I took the ridiculous suit to the hospital for Luke to see and left them in his room so he could look at them and remember drag racing. Later one of the nurses said to me, "We thought Luke was the drag racer?" It turned out Luke had been taking all the credit and telling the nurses he was a Nitro Harley rider! He was reeling off an extensive list of drag racing achievements – mostly mine. I later had to break the news to him that he wasn't the rider. Maybe he dreamed that he rode it, and who could blame him?

When he began talking again, Luke was also convinced he had a career as a nurse, which had been inspired by the people around him when he was in a coma. Psychologists at the hospital were asking him questions to track his recovery and when they asked what his occupation was he started to rattle on about doing his nursing apprenticeship – which was ridiculous of course because there was no such thing as a nursing apprenticeship, but that didn't stop him. What was more interesting was that he began to list all the things the nurses had been doing to him while he had been in a coma. There was no list he could have read to know these things, and no one had told him what had been happening, so the only way he knew was through listening to the nurses around him while he was supposed to be unconscious. It was fascinating and the nurses said he was getting it right, except Luke was telling the story as if he had been caring for himself. The way Luke remembered these events and conversations between nurses while he was in a coma gave me validation for my choices; he was aware of life around him in his coma, even if he didn't show responses. He heard what was going on around him, good or bad, and I was so glad we had been able to keep everything positive for him. We eventually had to give Luke the bad news that he wasn't a nurse, dropping hints that he was actually a mechanic and landscaper, and I felt a little bad. I didn't want to break the poor kid's heart because he seemed dead-set passionate about being a nurse.

I kept up the fresh faces and activities for Luke to trigger his memory. On his 21st birthday, we organised a big group burn-out with a bunch of bikes and Facetimed it live to him, stirring his memories about one of his favourite pastimes. My friend Sarah brought a whiteboard along and had everybody leave a special message for him and we placed the board in front of his hospital bed so he could read it over and over. This would help jog his mind about the people and relationships in his life.

Luke was in what the doctors called a curved recovery. Rapid progress was made early but as time went on and he grew closer to full health, the milestones grew further apart. Sometimes it seemed like not much was changing, but positive thinking remained my philosophy and I was defensive of Luke when that was challenged.

I had another drag race coming up in Darwin, the first round of the national championship. Shortly before I left for the trip, I had a disagreement with a doctor who had been talking with Mum. This doctor was very negative about Luke's future, which was causing excessive worry for Mum, who was more susceptible to that kind of talk. He said it was unlikely Luke would be walking or talking properly ever again. I understand everyone has a job to do and sometimes doctors keep expectations deliberately low, but this bloke was so overly down on Luke's future. He carried on like a clown and Mum listened, trusting his word. I had to give Mum an example of why Luke would be fine, so I asked her to listen when I told Luke to tell me the start up procedure was for a Nitro Harley.

He said, "To start the bike you pull the plugs out, check there is oil and fuel in the tank, then put air into the air tank. Whizz the bike over with the starter motor and check oil pressure and clear the motor of any fuel. Go through front and rear top dead centres and check pushrods, put the bike back to rear top dead centre, put the spark plugs in, hook the methanol up, make sure it is in second gear, fire the bike." He recited the whole process, start to finish. You could follow those steps exactly and you would have a running Nitro Harley. He even remembered a couple of things that I forgot (which I suppose is why he was the crew chief and I was the rider).

I said to Mum, "That is how to start a Nitro Harley, don't tell me he doesn't remember. I didn't tell him anything since his coma about starting the Harley, so let's get back to being positive and optimistic. Negativity breeds negativity."

I hadn't been back in Australia long before the Bahnmaier team from the USA got in touch with me again. They had a drag race on during the Sturgis Motorcycle Rally and wanted me to ride. Sturgis is legendary among motorcyclists the world over, and I had to make a split second decision in order to make it there in time, but I didn't need long to consider my answer. Luke was becoming more independent and aware by the day, Mum was on point in her care for him, and this trip would only take a few days.

I returned to the USA and flew into Kansas. Randy, one of my crew guys from the last trip, picked me up in his big Ford F-truck and he let me experience some more American freedom as we fired a bunch of amazing guns at his ranch. Randy's an ex-marine and he had some great stories about his time growing up in the Midwest and serving in the military. A lot of people say Kansas is boring, but I thought it had some really nice spots. There's a lot of drag racing out there – plenty of flat, open expanses of land helps.

To get to Sturgis in South Dakota we needed to make an 800 mile road trip in a rental car. Drew from the team joined us but he didn't know the way and left navigation to Randy, Randy's wife and I. We were having a good old time on the drive telling stories but not looking much at the map, and when we finally did pay attention we seemed to be getting further away from Sturgis rather than closer. We ended up on dirt roads and took all sorts of strange routes to try and get back in the right direction. I yearned for the beautiful mountain roads of Tennessee as we drove through barren Nebraska, a desolate state. We had no phone reception, so we couldn't even waste time on Facebook. We did see some bison on the side of the road as we drew closer to Sturgis and then the wildlife changed as we arrived in town after dark – becoming human and alcohol-fuelled.

I've seen a few parties in my life but I have never seen anything like Sturgis at night. The event attracts half a million riders to a small town that becomes the largest city in South Dakota for ten days. I thought back to Vegas, where the scale of the strip meant all the party animals were spread out, but at Sturgis everyone was in close quarters and it gave the feeling of a much busier place. Strange people and outfits milled among the crowds; one lady was wearing just a leather belt that covered a couple of strategic areas, and not much else. Saloon bars lined the streets and every one of them was overflowing with people.

I planned on enjoying the party soon enough but in the meantime we had a drag race to win. Sturgis Dragway wasn't like Bristol, this was an eighth mile track out in the countryside, with a narrow groove of rubber and rough concrete walls. It didn't have all the glitz and glamour of the big NHRA track but it still seemed like plenty of fun to me. When I looked at the track I thought it might be a tricky surface to get power to, but I walked on the start line and I found plenty of traction on the launching area. My team were clever and no doubt had a tune up to suit this strip. While I was away they had time to consider my body size and riding style and they had the bike dialled in real nice. By the third pass we were really cooking and we qualified second out of the eight bikes there. It was a nice feeling and I started to think it would be a mighty fine thing to take a trophy away from there.

We chilled out before round one of racing, not getting into the party atmosphere yet. This was a different scene to Bristol a few weeks previous, much more relaxed with a crowd more focused on where the next beer was coming from than the racing.

I was secretly hoping I would have some success at this meet. I came up against Freddie Robbins, another one of our team riders, in the first round. I had more cubic inches on board and thus more horsepower, but he really nailed the start and was ahead of me early. My bike didn't have a chance when it spun the tyre and went towards Freddie's lane. I had to get off the throttle and watch Freddy run away from me to the finish line and get the win. My racing was done for the day, but our team did well with Freddie getting a runner up in the Top Fuel class and the team owner Mike getting a win in the Pro Drag class. Their knowledge of Nitro Harleys was awesome, they were very safe to work around and they were always there to help me. I was very thankful for the weekend and tried to absorb as much information as possible from their experience.

After the race, the team said we had a few more obligations to fulfil. Out first stop was a veterans club, where they had a bingo night. I got to help out with calling the bingo, where everyone loved my accent and my smart-ass remarks. Later we took the bike to the Iron Horse Saloon, a real zoo of a bar with a massive stage and pit, surrounded by balconies on all sides. We were just there to display, but never ones to turn down an audience, we pitched the idea of a burnout and the owners were happy to oblige. We had a small bitumen area to work with which made it a little tricky, because the front tyre was sliding too much to really get the back tyre smoking. Still, we filled the place with nitro fumes and I was able to make a bit of noise and keep the people happy.

Afterwards I sat on the balcony and enjoyed some quiet Jack Daniel's and Cokes as I watched thousands of bikes ride past. Never in my life had I seen so many riders, from all different walks of life. Bikes glimmered as far as I could see on the main street, and I realised how lucky I was to be in this place, to still be alive and living a dream. I thought about how far from home I was, and how my life had changed in a few short years. I reflected on the love for my brother and my desire for him to fully recover, so he could experience this too. It was true that I was as wild as ever when it came to riding motorbikes and enjoying life, but I was also a changed man, with new priorities and responsibilities.

Finish Line

I flew home from Sturgis, and Luke had completely changed again. This time I found him in the gym where he could walk a couple of steps, stand for periods of time and transfer himself from benches to chairs. It was pleasing to hear him talking more like an adult; we were out of the worst stage and the rehabilitation could now begin. Only two days later he was discharged from hospital.

One of our first stops after Luke's release was an open day for my racing sponsor Hi-Tec Oils, where we had a burnout exhibition with my bike. He was walking around stiffly and slowly, but he was aware of what we were doing and I let him give the throttle a couple of revs. He didn't have the strength yet to really wrench it, so I put my hand over his and helped him give the throttle a few whacks, putting a smile on his face.

Luke's progress had been admirable. He knew the value of his physiotherapy and was working hard to rebuild his body. If there is something I've learned, it's that the body has a massive and amazing capacity for healing. Once I was through the dangerous, early stages of my own trauma, my recovery was in my hands, as was Luke's. He could choose to be miserable, swallowing more painkillers and cursing life, or he could work hard and build strength back, because life didn't have to disappear so easily.

Luke and I still had to deal with a thorn in the side as the next-of-kin hearing was coming up. The tribunal had taken weeks to organise, but those weeks meant a massive change in how the hearing was held, as Luke was now talking independently and able to give his opinion. The trial had been weighing on my mind, as even though Luke was out of hospital it was important for him to have somebody who understood what he was going through on his side while his recovery continued.

I had been on the bad side of judges in the past, but judges are good at taking every case on its own merits. Luke explained in court how he wanted me as his next-of-kin and the judge saw the stability in his mind, and liked how I had my own business and could support Luke. Dad didn't turn up for the hearing and the judge could see it wasn't in Luke's interests to make a change to the next-of-kin arrangement we had signed on his first night in hospital.

At the end of the hearing I was assigned as Luke's guardian for two years.

Luke's progress continued at home. He went through a lot of occupational and speech therapy, focusing on getting himself back to pre-accident condition, and while he was deemed as physically disabled, mentally he was almost back to 100 per cent. Sometimes he struggled with little things, like his focus might waver or he might not realise a simple mistake until after it was made, but considering how far he had come, those were little things I couldn't complain about. He even found himself a girlfriend, and because she worked away she could see improvements every couple of weeks when she returned. There were times when he was self conscious of his physical changes and I had to remind him of what he had accomplished, and what he had survived. Some people don't get a second chance at life – he was lucky enough to have his.

"How do you think I feel when I take my leg off in front of a bunch of kids before I hop into the pool?" I told him. "You still have your body and you still have your brain and you are going to be alright."

I know Luke looks at his life differently since his accident. I asked him what he was thinking when he first woke up from his coma. He said he knew he was there in the hospital, but he was trapped, with the lonely thought of, "Why the fuck am I like this?" I've been through some scary times, but I can't imagine his fear at that moment. I didn't want to lose my brother so I needed to be strong for him.

What is going to happen will happen, and maybe that's a futile outlook, but there are situations I can not change no matter how much I scream or cry. I can tear up and feel sad but staying that way doesn't help me or my loved ones. My future happiness, and those of the people I care about, is dependent on my actions. I aim to make every action one of growth and improvement for myself or for others.

Everything I did for Luke was a result of my personal experiences; for once it was me looking from the outside-in on a recovery. When I fought cancer, what I learned helped me deal with losing my leg, and what I learned in my accidents and amputation gave me the experience to help steer Luke's recovery. Experience is a tremendous teacher. There are people that will see my actions differently, as cold or pig-headed, but I will not apologise for being my brother's keeper.

Helping Luke allowed me to see a greater reason for the trials of life I had been through. I'm no oil painting, visually or morally, and I have had some brutal experiences in this life. But I still get up and go to work everyday and there is nothing I fear. My past experiences speak for me and my future experiences are consequences of my actions.

Fuel for Thought - IV
Epilogue

The interviews for this book took place throughout 2018. Later in the year I had a falling out with Luke and I think it's important for me to reconcile the experience with you honestly. I was travelling to Houston for a race and he wanted to get an operation done at the same time. I wanted him to wait until I got back so I could be there in case something went wrong and he didn't want to wait. He went to live with Mum and Dad again and that was his decision on what would be best for him. I moved to Queensland and Luke and I recently drove across the country in a truck together, which gave us the chance to have some good heart-to-hearts.

Everybody has their own journey and what works for me may not work for you; I say what I think and that can get me into trouble. Sometimes there is a need to tread lightly and if I tell someone they are going the wrong way when really they are just taking a different path, then I'm the negative presence in their life. I wouldn't change how I managed Luke's accident and in time we will find our way back to the strong relationship as brothers I know we are capable of.

My relationship with Dad remains at arm's length. We exchange occasional text messages but that is about it. He will tell me good luck for my racing, but I have a hard time being gracious when I think back to the rocky times we went through as father and son. He gave me a lot, but he also took a lot from me personally. I'm not sure if our relationship will ever be close, but perhaps civil is the best I can hope for.

Two years after Shanti Town's Nitro Circus party I paid off the fine, and there's a reason I was able to clear it so soon. I received a lump sum payment after my leg was amputated in order to pay for ongoing medical costs and prosthetics for the rest of my life. I used that payment to finalise my liabilities to the City of Armadale. Shanti Town literally cost me a leg.

I do a lot of public speaking now. Never, ever in my wildest dreams did I think I would be standing up in front of a high school or university and giving a speech on what I have been through. I love sharing my story, to see the look on people's faces. I've had people in fits of laughter and crying all in one speech. It's a new found passion and has even taken me back into the hospital to talk with new nurses. I like to tell them how the positive nurses during my recovery were so important – they were saints.

In a rare example of caution, I decided to sell my street bike (a toy I haven't mentioned in these pages until now). I weave in between cars and speed around and truthfully I love to do it, but it will only be a matter of time before a driver is texting or someone pulls out in front of me and cleans me up. When I was in hospital, I met many people in there from motorcycle accidents and maybe three quarters of them were caused by other people, and I realised I was just too silly to have a street bike.

Since I've met Tara I have settled down a lot and I'm starting to think more about the consequences of my actions. In the risk-reward calculation, the risks of a street bike seemed to be mounting, so I'm going to call it.

I'm doubling down on the Nitro Harley though and I bought a new race bike. I know the dangers involved but the difference on the race track is that I control the risk. I'm going to keep pursuing records and Aaron Deery might let me race his dragster soon to go after the outright world record for a drag racing amputee. I'd also love to do Bonneville one day and become the world's fastest amputee in any motorsport.

I was once told by a very wise friend of mine that we all end up in a grave with a headstone, and our life is reduced to a dash between two dates. It's what we do with the dash that counts – live your dash.

www.ingramcontent.com/pod-product-compliance
Lightning Source LLC
Chambersburg PA
CBHW050309010526
44107CB00055B/2172